And He Did Have Something to Say

Our Story of
Rev. Rufus King Young, Sr

Ellen Arneatha Verdia Young Fizer

 iUniverse®

AND HE DID HAVE SOMETHING TO SAY
OUR STORY OF REV. RUFUS KING YOUNG, SR

iUniverse books may be ordered through booksellers or by contacting:

iUniverse
1663 Liberty Drive
Bloomington, IN 47403
www.iuniverse.com
844-349-9409

Because of the dynamic nature of the Internet, any web addresses or links contained in this book may have changed since publication and may no longer be valid. The views expressed in this work are solely those of the author and do not necessarily reflect the views of the publisher, and the publisher hereby disclaims any responsibility for them.

Any people depicted in stock imagery provided by Getty Images are models, and such images are being used for illustrative purposes only. Certain stock imagery © Getty Images.

ISBN: 978-1-6632-0832-3 (sc)
ISBN: 978-1-6632-0833-0 (e)

Library of Congress Control Number: 2020916762

Print information available on the last page.

iUniverse rev. date: 08/31/2020

Contents

Dedication

Growing up in the south as a 'Pastor's Kid' provided for some interesting times. And although everyone knew who our father was, we grew up in a time when it really didn't matter what your parents did. We were all just African American children and young people trying to find our place and making it the best way we could. When everyone else was trying to tell us our place, some of us were very fortunate to have parents and teachers who encouraged and guided us to be whatever we wanted to be. My parents served the role of both parents and educators.

My father was a great story teller, and he would tell one story about a revival that he and my mother attended. The revival preacher was one of those who could really get the congregation on their feet. He was whooping and hollering, and the people were screaming and shouting. This went on for some time, and at the end of the evening everyone was spiritually filled and physically exhausted. Everyone left the revival that evening feeling like the Holy Spirit had been in that place that evening.

On the ride home, my mother kept repeating, "My Lord, that man could really preach." After saying this for the third or fourth time, she then added, "If he only had something to say." Daddy always said that one day he would write a book and the title of it would be, *'If He Only Had Something to Say.'*

Daddy, this is for you!

Acknowledgments

To all African American writers who have had the foresight and courage to write and publish your families' stories. You have been my inspiration, for our stories need to be told.

This story would not be possible if it were not for my siblings, the Younguns – Essie Mae, Rufus, Jr., James Robert and Allena. Although many times when we reflect on the past, we all may have slightly different versions of what actually happened. What is contained in this book is my truth. So, to my brothers and sisters I say thank you for all of the memories. And though Rufus Jr. has gone on before us, his presence will be felt in all future memories yet to come.

To my mother, Essie Mae Adams Young, the woman behind the man, the quiet, unassuming one, I will always be grateful to you for love, support, encouragement and life itself. You were the glue that held this family together. And even though you went home to glory over thirty-five years ago, I still feel your love surrounding me every day and encouraging me to do what you always knew I could do.

Special thanks go to my husband, Tyrone, and my daughters Shelby and Selena. Tyrone never questioned the countless hours I spent on the computer, although I am sure he wondered what I was doing. Shelby, my erudite daughter, has provided her special expertise in the initial editing of this book. And Selena, who as a child was my running buddy, continues to run with me.

I wish to also acknowledge my grandsons, Omavi and Quincy,

who are the joy of my life. This story is written primarily for them and generations of Younguns yet to be born.

And to all my friends and church members who have been asking over the years, *"When are you going to write or finish that book?"* Thank you for the pushing and constant nagging (you know who you are).

Finally, but foremost, to the one who makes all things possible, and the one to whom I give all honor and praise, to my Heavenly Father, who I know has watched over and protected this family throughout the years.

Jesus my Saviour
Who died for my sins
Gave his own life
My salvation to win.

Open the pearly gates
And bid me come in.

He is the Saviour for me!
He is the Saviour for me!

He is my way and I'm glad I can say,
He is the Saviour for me!

Written by Reverend Rufus King Young, Sr.

Preface

I was born November 17, 1948 in Jackson, Mississippi. Although my mother grew up in Jackson and my parents did live there at one point, Jackson was not their home at the time of my birth. Like my three siblings before me, my mother always returned to her mother in Jackson for the birth of her children.

I was the fourth of five children born to Rufus King Young, Sr. and Essie Mae Adams Young. Even though my birth certificate only states Ellen Arneatha, my father always told me my full name was Ellen Arneatha Verdia.

All of Rufus King and Essie Mae's children were named after a family member. My oldest sister was named after my mother – Essie Mae; my father's mother – Laura; and my mother's mother (middle name) – Elizabeth. Essie Mae Laura Elizabeth, whom we called Emley, was the first born (August 29, 1942). We often teased Emley that my parents gave her all the names just in case they could not have any more children. But that was not the case. My oldest brother was named after my father, Rufus King, Jr. (born December 17, 1943). Next was James Robert (born September 17, 1946), named after my mother's father and my father's father. I was named after one of my father's first cousins, Ellen Verdia Brooks Fontaine, who helped raise my father and his sister. Although a cousin, we always lovingly referred to her as Aunt Ellen. My youngest sister, Allena Anne (born April 26, 1951), was named after my father's grandfather – Allen with an "A" added to the end to make it feminine; and it is believed that the name Anne was after a dear church member at Visitors Chapel AME Church in Hot Springs, Miss Anne Smith.

Allena was the only one of us not born in Jackson. I don't know if it was because my mother did not have time to make it back to Jackson before she went into labor, or after four children my mother thought she could do this one without her mother. I've also heard the story that when it was near time for Allena to be born and my mother asked my father to return to Mississippi. My father's response was "NO – this time if you want to go home to have this baby, you go alone." Therefore, Allena was born in Hot Springs, Arkansas where my father was pastoring Visitors Chapel AME Church.

Growing up we called Emley 'Sister', and Rufus, Jr. 'Brother', and James Robert 'Budsy'. By the time it got to me and Allena, we were just called by our proper names. I guess they had run out of nicknames. However, my father sometimes called me 'papoose' because he said when I was born, I looked like a little Indian baby. My father referred to his five children as the "Younguns". During the Christmas season, he would send out a holiday letter to family, friends and his congregation updating them on his children. He would always sign the letters – *Rev. & Mrs. R.K. Young and the Younguns.*

By the time we reached adulthood all nicknames had been dropped. We were all properly named, for we were all the proper children of the Reverend Rufus King Young, Sr., and this is our story, although mostly about Daddy for he was the real hero or *Superstar* of the family. And, when he spoke, he always had something to say. This is the story of our lives growing up with the *Right Reverend R. K. Young.*

Reverend Rufus King Young, Sr.

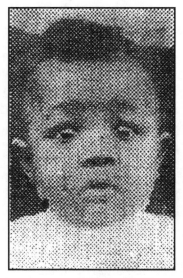

A very young Rufus K. Young

I was recently asked, what it was like growing up as a preacher's kid. I found it very difficult to answer this question because my upbringing was what it was, and I really didn't know any other way of existence. As I look back on it, there may have been many restrictions placed on the R. K. Young children, but my childhood was full of so many fond memories.

My father, Rev. Rufus King Young, Sr., helped to create many of those memories. So, who was this man who was admired and revered by all who knew him? Some called him a righteous man.

Others called him a caring pastor; a civil rights activist. And still others referred to him as a local hero of his time – a man who stood for what was right in the sight of God. But Emley, Rufus, Jr., James Robert, Allena and I just called him Daddy.

Rufus King Young was born May 13, 1911 in Drew County, Arkansas. His parents were Robert and Laura Scott Young. My father had an older half-brother by his father, Theodore Alexander Young. My father did not know his father very well because Robert died when my father was only four years old. Robert and Laura had two children together, my father and his sister, Bertha Maryann Estello Elizabeth Alice Young (Lewis), whom we called Aunt Bert. *(Now you can see where the long names came from.)* After my father's father died, his mother moved to Chicago and the rearing of my father and his sister fell into the hands of Robert's father, Allen Young and his second wife, Katie. My grandmother, Laura (whom we called MamMaw) went on to have another son, Clifton William Young.

Allen Young and his first wife, Mary Ann Bosley Young had eleven children: Nine boys – Gustavus, Sylvannus, King, Martin Van Buren, Robert, Meredith, Isaac, Green and James, who was the baby; and two girls, Ellen and Martha. Sylvannus later changed his name to Allen Wesley – we called him Uncle A.W. The story is that Uncle A.W. had a lisp and could not correctly say his name, Sylvannus; and therefore, when he became an adult, he legally changed his name.

Daddy would often tell us about his grandfather. Allen Young was born in 1844 in Mississippi as a slave. He was sold and taken to Tennessee and never saw his family again. He was set free in Texas in 1865 and traveled to Arkansas. Allen Young prayed for three things – freedom; a wife and family; and land. The Lord blessed him with all three – his freedom; a wife (actually two wives) and eleven children; and in 1877 he was deeded 160 acres of land.

My father and his sister grew up on his grandfather's farm in Drew County, Arkansas. His grandfather had acquired the land by homesteading. If one cleared the land, took possession and farmed the land, he/she ended up owning the land. The closest town was Dermott, which is about 115 miles southeast of Little Rock. It is in the middle of nowhere. Today the population of Dermott is less than 3,500. As an adult when I would return to Dermott it seems as if nothing much had changed; a few newer homes and churches, but mostly still farmland. Of course, I'm of the belief that most Americans probably could not have located the state of Arkansas on a U.S. map before Clinton became president - even after the notoriety of the *"Little Rock Nine"* in 1957. To this day my family still owns that farmland in Arkansas (now approximately 205 acres), which my father had incorporated in 1994 and it is now known as the Allen Young Estate, Inc.

All of the officers and shareholders of the Allen Young Estate, Inc are direct descendants of my great-grandfather. The by-laws for the corporation require that if one of the heirs wants to sell his/her shares, the other heirs must be given the right of first refusal. Based on this provision, my father at the time of his death owned the majority of the shares by purchasing the shares of those who wished to sell. Like his grandfather, the one thing my father treasured dearly was land ownership – something that belonged to you. When the farmland was first incorporated, there were ten family member shareholders. Today, all of the original shareholders are deceased, but the land is still owned by direct descendants of Allen Young.

Daddy always had fond memories of the farm and growing up there, especially with his sister and his cousin Ellen. My Aunt Bert would tell the story of when she was about four, Daddy was seven and Aunt Ellen was almost 17. She doesn't remember where the three of them had been, but they were on their way back to the farmhouse when Daddy got tired and refused to walk any further and just sat down in the road. Aunt Ellen begged and pleaded with him to get up and walk because it was beginning to get dark. Well, Aunt Bert, who loved her big brother and tried to emulate him in every way, decided if her brother was sitting down in the road then so would she. No matter what Aunt Ellen did, neither would budge. Aunt Ellen knew they would all get in trouble if they did not get home before dark, especially her being the oldest. So, with no other choice, she picked up my father and carried him several yards. Aunt Bert still refused to move. So, Aunt Ellen had to go back and pick her up and carried her to the spot where Daddy was. This back and forth relay continued all the way home.

Although the details are a little sketchy, it was also around this time that their mother did return and took my Daddy and Aunt Bert to live with her for a short period of time in East St. Louis. However, during those times, it was very difficult for a single mother of two to make it, so Daddy and Aunt Bert were returned to their grandfather and the farm.

But there was much joy and happiness on the farm. Aunt Bert says she remembers the day her brother was called to preach. She said they had been out in the field on the turn row just behind what she referred to as the "big house". She said Daddy said he heard God speak to him and tell him he was to preach and spread the word of God to all that would listen. Daddy was so excited as he explained to his sister what had happened. They both raced back to the big house to tell Grandpa Young who shouted for joy. You see, Allen Young had nine sons and he always wanted just one of them to become a minister. That did not happen, but he was realizing his dream through his grandson. Once the excitement died down, Aunt Bert said Grandpa asked her, "Well, God spoke to your brother, what did God say to you?" to which she replied, "God didn't say anything to me!"

Later in life Daddy said that one of the saddest days in his life on the farm was after his mother remarried to Albert Meekins and she came to the farm and took Aunt Bert back to live with her, her husband and younger brother, Clifton in Dermott. At the same time, Aunt Ellen left to attend college at Philander Smith College in Little Rock. Daddy said he remembers that as being one of the first times he really cried, because as he put it, he was left alone on the farm.

Aunt Ellen *(b. September 5, 1901, d. January 7, 2000)* went on to become a registered nurse, which was quite an accomplishment for a young black woman during those times. Aunt Ellen married William Fontaine, who owned a barber shop on Ninth Street in Little Rock. Aunt Ellen and Uncle Bill never had children. Aunt Bert *(b. October 25, 1914, d. February 13, 2017)* spent a long, satisfying career as an educator in the North Little Rock School system. For many years, Uncle A.W. was her principal. Aunt Bert married Jack Lewis, Sr. and they had three boys, Jack, Jr., Joseph Allen *(b. November 13, 1951, d. June 4, 2019)*, and Clifton Wesley. Jack, Joe and Cliff are my only first cousins. Neither of my father's half-brothers had children. My mother was an only child – well, until much later in life. I'll tell that story later.

Daddy received his early education at the Chicot County Training School in Dermott, AR. He then received his Associate of Arts Degree and Bachelor of Arts Degree from Shorter College in North Little Rock, AR; a Master's of Divinity Degree from Payne Theological Seminary at Wilberforce University, Wilberforce, Ohio; and continued with additional post-graduate studies at Chicago University.

Reverend Young was licensed to preach by the African Methodist Episcopal (AME) Church in 1924 at the age of 12 and received his first pastoral appointment at the age of 18. He was ordained an Elder in 1934 and pastored churches in Arkansas, Mississippi, Alabama and Louisiana. He met and married my mother, Essie Mae Adams, when he was pastoring Hair's Tabernacle in Jackson, Mississippi.

Daddy's graduation from Shorter College - 1935
R.K. Young is on the bottom row, first on the left.

The highest rank for a pastor in the African Methodist Episcopal Church is that of Itinerant Elder – the key word being 'itinerant'. An Itinerant Elder's pastoral assignment is only for one year. And, as the title implies, they may be required to travel from place to place; from church to church. That's exactly what my father did during the early years of his ministry. In addition to pastoring churches in Arkansas, Mississippi and Alabama, my father served for four years as the Dean of the School of Religion at Campbell College in Jackson, Mississippi (later acquired by Jackson State University); two years as President of Daniel Payne College in Birmingham, Alabama; and for many years as the Dean of the Jackson Theological Seminary, Shorter College in North Little Rock, Arkansas. He also taught at various colleges and public-school systems.

It was when my father was President of Daniel Payne College (1948 – 1950) that I was born. Although only six or seven at the time, Emley vividly recalls living on the college campus. The

President's home was being occupied by the AME Bishop of the Eighth Episcopal District, Bishop *Sherman L. Greene*. This was only to be temporary because Bishop Greene was having a home built in an exclusive area for Blacks in Birmingham, Alabama. So, during his presidency, my father and his family lived in an upstairs apartment like area of the Student Union building on campus.

Emley says that there was a great deal of racial tension in Birmingham at the time due to the movement to register Blacks to vote. My father was out that evening working for the cause of social justice, for he has always been a civil rights activist. My mother, Emley, Rufus, Jr., James Robert and I (a small infant at the time) were in the upstairs apartment when the Ku Klux Klan came on campus to terrorize the students. My mother turned off all the lights in the apartment and cradled us all around her on the floor. She was holding me in her lap and trying her best to quiet James Robert who was only two. The Ku Klux Klan were whooping and hollering outside and burned a cross on the lawn of the Student Union building. They then threw rocks and stones through the plate glass windows of the Student Union building before they rode off.

Bishop Greene never got to occupy his new home, for the KKK bombed his house and all of the other exclusive homes for Blacks. It was not until much later in her life that Emley realized the seriousness of that situation and what danger we would have encountered had they entered the building or set it on fire. However, Emley says she never felt frightened because Mommy was there.

For a little over a year (1950 -1951) my father pastored St. Paul AME Church in Montgomery, Alabama. It was here that Rosa Parks was one of his parishioners. This, of course, was prior to her 1955 historic refusal to give up her seat on a public bus to a white man, which lead to the Montgomery Bus Boycott. I am told that Ms. Parks would watch James Robert and I during the Sunday Worship services as my father preached and my mother sang in the choir. My father and Mrs. Park communicated over the years and she was one of the recipients of those famous Christmas letters signed Rev. and Mrs. R. K. Young and the Younguns.

During his early days as a pastor in Arkansas, Rev. Young pastored churches in Lake Village, Gaines Landing, Parnell, Baxter, and Collins. In 1940 he was assigned outside of his home state and did not return to Arkansas until 1951 when he became pastor of Visitors Chapel in Hot Springs. It was the summer of 1953 when he was assigned to Bethel African Methodist Episcopal Church in Little Rock, Arkansas (12th Episcopal District), and there he spent the next 33 years as senior pastor.

As a Pastor

Rev. Rufus King Young, Sr. was the type of pastor who cared deeply about each of his parishioners. I categorize Daddy as a teaching preacher. His objective was to make the scriptures come alive and remain relevant in your life. He wanted to make sure you understood the word of God.

Rev. Young would personally provide communion to every sick and shut-in member of his church. On the first Monday of each month you did not have to ask where Rev. Young was. He would pick up one of two of the Deaconess of the church, and they were off to visit with and provide Holy Communion to those members of the church who were unable to get out. Providing communion to the sick and shut-in was an all day, sometimes two-day labor of love; and the members looked forward to these monthly visits. (A Deaconess in the AME Church is defined as a woman selected by the Pastor and the official board of the church and consecrated by the Bishop. Her duties include providing special needs to the fallen, hungry, homeless, imprisoned or institutionalized... *The Doctrine and Discipline of the African Methodist Episcopal Church – 2016: The Bicentennial Edition, published by order of the Fiftieth General Conference of the AME Church, AME Church Publishing House, Nashville, TN.)*

Rev. Young has been described by his congregants as a mentor and a spiritual leader – one who instilled Christian values in his members. In 2013 on the occasion of Bethel AME Church's 150th Anniversary, the late Annette Roper, who along with her sister M. Eartha Daniel chaired the 150th Anniversary events, of Rev. Young said the following, "He was soft-spoken, very meek and humble; but he despised discrimination... He took a stand when a lot of people wouldn't, especially black people."

In the 2001 award winning documentary *We Shall Not Be Moved*, Ernest Green, one of the Little Rock Nine and the first African American to graduate from Central High School in 1958, states, "Without our faith and our beliefs...we would not have made it through. Rev. Young was one of the ministers who stood up. The NAACP would meet at Bethel Church." Later, in September 2017, at a Church School program held at Metropolitan AME Church in Washington, D.C. commemorating the 60th anniversary of the desegregation of Central High School, Ernest Green said, "Rev. Young was an exceptional person and pastor. He was not afraid to stand up for what he believed was right when so many others would not. Rev. Young and Bethel AME Church will always have a special place in my heart."

Also, in the 2001 documentary, another of the Little Rock Nine, Melba Patillo Beals adds that Bethel was her home, her sanctity, her only hope of safety. And Mr. Charlie Boykins, who at the time was an officer and member of Bethel states, "He (Rev. Young) was more than just a pastor here at Bethel. He was an organizer; he was a builder; and he was a facilitator."

Daddy also felt it was his role to mentor and nurture young adults who were aspiring to become ministers. Among those that he tutored were the late Rev. James H. Cone, Ph.D. *(1938 – 2018)* the noted scholar, theologian, professor, author, and best known as the father of Black Theology); and his brother, the late Rev. Cecil W. Cone, Ph.D. *(1937 – 2016)* also a theologian, pastor and educator. Daddy was also one of the first pastors during his time to welcome women into his pulpit. At the time, my mother even questioned the wisdom of allowing women this sacred right. Rev. Marla Coulter-McDonald, who is now the Network Director for Spiritual Care and Chaplaincy Services in Indianapolis, IN and who was one of the guest speakers for Bethel's 155th Anniversary in 2018 referred to Daddy as her father in the ministry. I can remember when Rev. Marla as a very young person first entered the pulpit at Bethel AME Church under the watchful and caring eyes of my father.

Upon my father's death, one of the self-proclaimed "Bethel Younguns", LaRouth Smith Perry, PhD, wrote to Emley, James Robert, Allena and me stating that she remembered my father as, "a brilliant Bible scholar, a pastor's pastor, the Shorter College lecturer, a sincere church pastor, a gentle disciplinarian, a thorough listener, and a gardener." Dr. Perry proclaimed that Little Rock and Bethel would never be the same since God called Rev. Young from labor to reward.

Rev. R.K. Young
Speaking from the pulpit at Bethel A.M.E. Church in 2003

As a Father

Growing up it seemed as though Daddy was always at the church or about church business. My mother taught the five of us to respect our father, and that we did; at least most of the time. I was the one who always seemed to talk back or ask the difficult questions. Sometimes I believe the others would put me up to confronting Daddy with something they were afraid to ask him. Daddy would always listen.

Daddy took his responsibility of taking care of his family seriously. My Daddy would tell the story of when he was first assigned to Bethel AME Church in Little Rock. He said several of the congregants were hesitant about a pastor with five children and made comments like, "We've never had a Pastor with that many children. What are we going to do with all of them children?" To which my Daddy responded in his usual slow and deliberate manner, "I don't expect *you* to do anything with them children. Your job is to take care of me and pay me, and I will take care of my own children."

To the rest of the world he was a dynamic preacher, a community leader, a civil rights activist, an advocate for human rights and social justice, a gentle giant. But to us, he was just Daddy. For as long as I can remember, up until well past his retirement, Daddy would get up every morning and put on a suit, dress shirt and tie. His wardrobe would not be complete without his suspenders. He dressed this way even on the weekends. I guess he never knew when one of his members or someone may need him and he wanted to always be prepared to go in a moment's notice. He always had a persona about him as being very serious minded and always about the business at hand – *God's business*. At home, we saw another man, a much more relaxed and fun- loving man.

Rev. and Mrs. R.K. Young and the Younguns - 1958
Left to Right: James Robert, Rufus Jr., Daddy,
Allena, Mommy, Emley, Ellen

Daddy Stories

Emley says she can recall several occasions when she and Rufus Jr. (and probably James Robert) were small. When they would arrive home from church at night, Daddy would jump out of the car before anyone else and race into the dark house. Daddy would be hiding somewhere in the dark house, and when they entered, he would jump out and go *"BOO"*. Even though they knew he was going to try and scare them, they were always startled. Daddy would never tire of this little trick and they would never cease to be scared to death. But then they would always laugh, because once again Daddy had gotten one over on them. (Years later James Robert would play the same trick on me and Allena. I guess I know where he got it from - he acquired the talent honestly.)

Rufus Jr. always had a great deal of respect for Daddy. However, of the five of us, Rufus Jr. was the prankster, the fun loving one, the one who could make anyone laugh and always kept us laughing.

There were times, however, when Rufus Jr. would get so angry with Daddy – probably because Daddy wouldn't let him do what he wanted to do; which probably was not a good thing to do anyway. After Rufus Jr. went away to college, he came back with a new vocabulary, and when he got angry with Daddy, he would call him *"an old Bajanja Head"*. Of course, never to his face and always out of Daddy's hearing range. I never knew what a Bajanja was – I assume it was just a made-up word Rufus Jr. used in the place of profanity – which of course, was not allowed in our house. Later we would lovingly refer to Daddy at times as Bajanja Head and Daddy always had some sort of a comical retort, like calling us pumpkin head or squash head.

James Robert's fondest memories of Daddy are his wit, and though not "quick" comebacks, nevertheless were witty comebacks. James Robert recalls when he was going through his radical phase and was a strong believer that everything was relative. One day he said in Daddy's presence that, "THERE ARE NO ABSOLUTES". After a moment to reflect on what his son had just said, Daddy responded – "Well, that was an ABSOLUTE!" James Robert could only go – "Hmmmmm." On another occasion James Robert and Daddy arrived home to find that wasps had built a nest in the carport and they were both buzzed by wasps when they got out of the car. James Robert declared that he was going to knock the nest down; to which Daddy cautioned him not to because he could get stung. James Robert, being the big, brave man retorted – "I'm not scared, I can out run those wasps." To which Daddy calmly replied, "Yeah, but can you out fly them?"

Ellen (I) remembers Saturday mornings, when as children we would gather around the TV and watch cartoons, as most kids did at the time. There were no computers, video games, tablets or the like. Daddy was not able to join us much for this Saturday morning ritual, but when he did it was a thrill. Daddy had a laugh that would come from deep down within him and it seemed to shake the room. It normally started out like a loud whoop as he would inhale air and ended up like a cackling sound made in the back of his throat as he exhaled the air in a staccato like sound. The laugh is hard to describe, but it was unmistakable – you had to hear it to believe it. His laugh was infectious and would literally make you laugh too, regardless of whether the situation was funny or not. On those occasions when he did spend a few minutes watching cartoons with us, he would laugh so hard that we would stop watching the television and just watch Daddy enjoying himself. I will never forget that laugh.

We grew up in an era when cowboys and westerns reigned supreme on television. Shows like Gunsmoke, The Rifleman, Bat Masterson, Have Gun Will Travel, Bonanza, Big Valley, Wyatt Earp, Roy Rogers, Cisco Kid, Maverick, and Cheyenne were quite popular. Westerns dominated the TV screen during the 50's and 60's. While viewing one of our favorite westerns, starring on the show was none other than Sammy Davis, Jr, a Black man, all decked out with a cowboy hat, a holster with gun and spurs on his cowboy boots. Now, James Robert, Allena and I thought this was hilarious – who ever heard of a Black cowboy. I remember a heated discussion ensued because James Robert and I were convinced there were no such things as Black cowboys – after all, we had never seen any on television before. Daddy laughed at us because he thought we were absolutely ridiculous. In his calm manner he asked us – "Do cowboys ride horses?" – To which we answered *yes*. Daddy said, "Well, I rode a horse." Then he asked – "Do cowboys shoot guns?" – Again, the answer was *yes*. "Well, I shot a gun." Finally, he asked – "Do cowboys herd cows?" Of course, we responded. To which Daddy simply replied – "Well, I herded cows. Then I guess that makes me a cowboy." We were still not convinced.

Several years later when I was a freshman at Fisk University, my first job on the federal work-study program was in the campus library. The old library at Fisk was referred to as *the castle*. Part of my job was placing books back on the shelves after students had returned them. One night as I was busy about my task, I was picking up a book from the cart to return to its proper place on the shelf, when I happened to glance at the title - *"Black* Cowboys". I couldn't believe my eyes. I spent the next few minutes skimming through the book and looking at names and pictures of Black cowboys like William "Bill" Pickett, Stagecoach Mary, Nat Love and Bass Reeves, among others. I could not wait to get back to the dorm that evening so I could call home to tell my Dad he was right. Daddy only laughed. Today I realize that I should have known he was right all along – he always was.

Just as a point of information, in 1994 the United States Post Office in its Legends of the West series honored two of perhaps the most notable black cowboys – Jim Beckwourth (mountain man, fur trader and explorer); and Bill Pickett (cowboy and rodeo performer).

One of the best pieces of advice I ever received in life came from none other than my father. When I was in high school, a classmate had invited several of us to his church one Sunday. I do believe they may have been celebrating Youth Sunday. Even though it was a Baptist Church – church is church, especially for a teenager. We were invited for the entire day, Sunday School and morning worship. Although I don't remember the subject or the scripture reference for the Sunday School lesson, I do recall being confused by something we had read in the scripture and began to question it. The very serious and well-meaning Sunday School teacher looked at me in disbelief and said, "We don't question what is in the Bible." Being the obedient, well-behaved, young person, my parents had raised me to be, I did not pursue the matter with this adult. Later that evening, I relayed the incident to my father. His response to me was that you question anything you don't understand. You may not always come to a complete understanding at that time; or the explanation given may still not make sense to you. But you never stop seeking to understand. That piece of advice has become the mantra for my life. I now know that there are many things in the Bible that are beyond my understanding, even at this age. But as my father taught me – I *never stop seeking to understand.*

Allena, being the baby of the family probably has more *Daddy Stories* than anyone. Of the three girls, she is perhaps the biggest daddy's girl and there may be a reason for that. I told you that Allena was the only one of the Younguns not born in Jackson. She also has the esteem honor of being the only one of us in which Daddy was actually in the delivery room when she was born. Mommy and Daddy both told her the story that when Mommy was in the delivery room and Daddy was in the waiting room, one of the attendants rushed into the waiting room to ask Daddy to quickly come into the delivery room because they needed help calming Mommy down. Daddy was scrubbed up and told to put on the traditional operating room scrubs. Once inside the delivery room, Daddy did all he could to calm Mommy. It was a difficult labor and when Allena started to appear in this world it was feet first. They quickly had to get another doctor, an Asian physician with smaller hands, to actually go in and turn the baby around. So well before Lamaze became popular, Daddy coached his wife through the delivery of what would be their last child.

Allena's favorite Daddy story took place when she was small and Daddy would stand at the door of the Old Bethel on Ninth and Broadway in Little Rock to greet and shake hands with his parishioners as they would leave the Sunday service. Allena remembers standing there with Daddy and playing and twirling around in his long robe. Often times she would get to shake hands too. Allena recalls that even after we moved to the new church, she would still stand with Daddy at the end of the service, although maybe too big then to play in his robe, the desire to do so was still there.

As I said, we were taught to respect our father. When he came home, he was the king of the house and it was our job to make him comfortable. So, on Sunday nights when we would return home from all day church, we would rush and get Daddy's slippers (or house shoes as we called them) and help him put them on. Our reward for doing so was to be able to stand on Daddy's feet and have him dance around the room carrying us on his feet. *(How true are the words of the late Luther Vandross – Oh, just to dance with my father again.)*

Daddy took pride in all of our accomplishments. The expectation was that we would do well, so there was no need to continuously verbalize this. We were rewarded for our good grades. Daddy would give us a dime for every "A" on our report card and a nickel for every "B". There was no reward for anything below a B because that would have been below expectation. Education was held in high regard in the Young household. There was never a question as to whether or not you were going to college after high school graduation. In fact, I believe Daddy personally drove all five of his Younguns to college their freshman year.

Speaking of going off to college, I have to interject this story about Mommy. If Mommy had had her way, I think none of her children would have ever grown up and they certainly would have never moved away from home. Every time one of us would leave for college it was a heartbreaking experience for Mommy. After Daddy had packed up the car and all the goodbyes had been said, Mommy would always run and lock herself in the bathroom. She did not want to see her *babies* leave. We could hear her crying on the other side of the bathroom door, but she refused to come out until she knew we were gone and the car was out of sight. She would not accompany my father on these *going to college* trips either. I know when I left for Fisk University, my Aunt Ellen rode with my father and me to Nashville. Aunt Ellen would say to Mommy, "Good Lord Essie, they're just going to college, not off to war."

The R.K. Young Household

I wish those days could come back once more,
I wish those days never had to go.
I loved them so.

Stevie Wonder

For those of you who think or have heard that the South moves at a slower pace, you are correct. Those of us who grew up in the South and then moved North, East or West know this to be true. After having lived on the east coast for over 40 years, I am often told that I still have a southern drawl, particularly with certain words. Although I would like to think I don't sound quite so southern anymore. When I reflect on my childhood, I do think of a much more relaxed and not so hurried lifestyle.

One thing was certain, you could never rush or hurry my father. My father chewed every mouthful of food exactly 50 times before swallowing. Brushing his teeth was a major production. Each brush stroke was slow and meticulous, with just the right up and down and sideway motions. His thought process also seemed to be slow, yet deliberate. We would often joke that you could ask my father a question, eat dinner, go outside and play, do your homework, and then, MAYBE, he was ready to answer you. And nine times out of ten the answer was, "go ask your mother." Little did we know that his thought process was not slow, but actually much faster than that of most people. I think he took his time to speak so that he could carefully choose the words. He wanted to make sure that what he said was clearly understood by all, for he definitely had something to say.

It was a slow-paced life, but we enjoyed every minute. Life didn't seem to pass you by so quickly, and the good times seemed to have lasted much longer. Growing up as a PK (preacher's kid) had advantages and disadvantages. My mother was constantly reminding us that we couldn't do this or we couldn't go there because we were Rev. Young's kids. I recall when I was 18 years old and was presented as a debutante at the Alpha Phi Alpha Debutante Ball (Christmas of 1966), my father could not escort me to the gala as the other young debutantes' fathers did. This would have been considered inappropriate for my father to be anywhere that served alcohol. But it was okay for his daughter to be presented into society at this occasion. So, I was escorted by my father's younger brother, Clifton Young.

All of my early childhood memories in Little Rock are fond ones. My father went to work every day at the church. He spent a great deal of time visiting and communing with the sick and shut-in and attending to other church and civic duties. My mother taught in the public-school systems, first in the Pulaski County School District, then the Little Rock School System and finally the North Little Rock School system. Mommy would always come home from work and prepare a nice hot meal, which always consisted of a meat, at least two vegetables, hot cornbread, and in season, a fresh garden salad. And don't forget the big pitcher of Kool-Aid. Normally, it was my job to make the Kool-Aid. We would always eat dinner together and then my father would return to the church for some type of board/church meeting.

My mother always called my father "Reverend"; and my father called my mother "Baby". Most of the rearing of the children was left to my mother. As I look back on it, I wonder how she was able to handle a full-time job, five children, a husband, most of the housework and cooking, in addition to her duties as "first lady" of Bethel AME Church, which she did with dignity and grace.

The Parsonage – the House on Ringo Street

I was four years old when my family moved to Little Rock (did not turn 5 until that November). But I do remember when we moved into the parsonage that was located at 2304 Ringo Street in Little Rock. The house was owned by the church. The first floor of the two-story house had a living room to the right when you entered the front door; my father's study was to the left, which was filled with all of his 'religious' books. Continuing down the hallway, the dining room was to the left and the 'girls' bedroom was across the hallway. At the end of the hallway was a bathroom and stairs that led to the second floor, which was one large bedroom with a bathroom. The upstairs was the 'boys' room.

In the back of the house on the first floor was the kitchen and breakfast room to the left and my parents' bedroom in the very rear of the house. The master bedroom also had a bathroom. There was a small enclosed porch area in the rear of the house that connected my parents' bedroom to the breakfast room. An old washing machine sat on this back porch. The front of the house had a screened in front porch, with two or three chairs and a two-seater porch swing.

The house also had a large attic which you could enter from a long closet area in the 'boys' room. Part of the attic had flooring and we spent a great deal of time playing in the attic. Of course, this would only be when the boys – Rufus, Jr. and James Robert would allow us upstairs into their sanctuary. This is where we lived, and I do mean lived until I was ten years old.

Even though there are less than nine years between the oldest Youngun and the youngest Youngun, it seems that growing up it was just James Robert, Allena and me. Emley and Rufus, Jr. seemed to be so much older and were gone way too soon. I had not turned nine when Emley left for college. Rufus, Jr. spent his 11ᵗʰ grade in Jackson, Mississippi with my mother's parents because Governor Orval Faubus had closed all of the Little Rock public high schools to prevent any further integration.

James Robert, Allena and I spent countless hours playing in that backyard on Ringo Street. There was an old pecan tree that stood in the middle of the yard, which had long since passed its productive years. There was also an old rickety garage that was in much need of repair. Although my mother warned James Robert about climbing on top of that garage, he often did just for the fun of it.

Behind the house was an alley that separated the backyards of the houses on Ringo Street from the backyards of the houses on Cross Street. Most residents used the alley to access the backyards of their homes, which is where they usually parked their cars. This alley, often times became our playground.

Phyllis Carter, who was my age and an only child, lived down at the other end of the alley. She and her family were also members of Bethel AME Church. Phyllis would often have to slip off to come play at my house, so I spent a great deal of time playing on her back porch. She spent many hours at our house and I at hers. Phyllis was my best neighborhood friend. During those times I was envious of Phyllis because she developed physically much sooner than the rest of the girls our age.

The Mitchell family lived directly behind us and had one child, Otis. The Mitchell house faced 23rd Street, but their backyard opened into the alley. Otis and the boys who lived in the house behind the Mitchells always seemed to congregate in our backyard. These boys would also join James Robert in the illicit trips to the roof of the rickety garage.

There was always something going on in the backyard or up and down that alley. Through the eyes of a child that backyard seemed to be a mile long and wide. However, when I have returned as an adult, that yard seems so tiny and is hardly large enough for two cars. The old rickety garage has long since been torn down. And that old pecan tree no longer stands in the middle of the yard.

Also, in the backyard was a clothes line where Mommy would hang the wash that for years she washed by hand in the bathtub. One of our favorite pastimes was to take a running start, grab hold to one of the cross poles at the end of the clothes line and swing ourselves back and forth. We could entertain ourselves with this activity for hours. One day when I was about seven or eight, I took my running start and reached to grab hold of the pole. Because we had been playing for sometimes my hands were sweaty, and so was the pole. When I grabbed the pole, my hands slipped; my legs went forward and I landed hard on the ground on my back and the back of my head hit the ground. I don't remember much of what happened after that because I was unconscious. I can remember slightly coming into consciousness sometimes during the night. I was in my bed and my head was in my mother's lap and she was crying and praying; praying and crying. And then I drifted off again. I really don't know how long I remained unconscious. I was later told I had suffered a concussion and had vomited several times before I regained consciousness. Later, about the time I entered puberty, I would suffer from severe migraine headaches. In adulthood I was told by a neurologist that the headaches were as a result of a weakened blood vessel to the brain. My mother always believed that the headaches were directly related to that backyard accident. Today, that clothes line is also gone from the backyard on Ringo Street.

Mommy made sure her children never wanted for anything. I can remember when we were still in the house on Ringo Street and the *Whamo Hula-Hoops* were the biggest craze and we were dying to have one. At that time, we only had one car and of course it was in use most of the time by the Reverend on church business. My mother took the bus in the rain to go downtown to get her children hula-hoops. I guess she did it just to see the joy and excitement on our faces when she returned with them. We spent the rest of the day playing with our new toys on the front porch since the rain prevented us from going into the yard.

Mommy was the protective one; the cautious one; and yet the more perceptive one. Daddy was the risk taker; the outspoken one; the bold one. I say Mommy was perceptive because she knew what our gifts and talents were before we did. She could also predict with pretty good accuracy what my father would do and how he would react in certain situations. My father had great hopes that his firstborn son and name sake would follow in his footsteps and become a preacher. Mommy said she told my father very early on that Rufus, Jr. was not the one and that James Robert would be the one to become a minister. She was right.

It was in that house on Ringo Street that we got our first family pet, a black and white cocker spaniel given to us by my grandmother Laura's second husband Albert Meekins, whom we called Daddy Albert. Daddy Albert brought the frisky little puppy to us shortly after we arrived in Little Rock. Because of his black and white spots, we immediately called her Spotty. I was five when we got Spotty and she lived until I was a sophomore in college – almost 15 years.

Sundays and Church Life

Easter Sunday - 1958
Left to Right: Allena, Connie Smith, Ellen – on the
sidewalk on Ninth Street in front of Old Bethel A.M.E.
Church (Ninth & Broadway, Little Rock, AR)

All of our activities growing up were centered around the church. In the 50s and 60s there was not much else for children of color in Little Rock, Arkansas to do. We were involved in all youth church activities – the children's choir, which my mother was the pianist/director; the youth choir, which Mrs. Marlene Smith was the pianist/director; junior usher board, Young People's Department (YPD), Sunday School, ACE (Allen Christian Endeavor) League – which was the evening version of Sunday School, and Vacation Bible School. Even the Boy Scout and Girl Scout Troops were sponsored by the church. Ms. Lucille Scott was our YPD director as well as our Girl Scout Troop leader. For Rev. and Mrs. R.K. Young and the Younguns, Sundays were a day of church – and I do mean all day.

Our Sundays began with 9:30 am Sunday School; then 10:45 am Morning Worship Service; then there was normally a Tea or some other afternoon event at the church; then 6:00 pm ACE League; and finally, 7:30 Evening Worship Service. Many Sundays we would leave the house at 9:00 am and not return until 10:00 pm. And though I can remember complaining profusely, when I look back, I cherish those days.

Often times at the evening Worship Service there would be no one there but the Youngs, the Smiths and one or two others. L.N. Smith was one of the Stewards at Bethel. He and his wife, Marlene had four children, who were close in age to the Younguns. Their youngest daughter, Connie was my age (our birthdays are only 15 days apart) and because we were always at church, we became best church buddies.

During the summer after Vacation Bible School, Connie and I were given permission to walk from the church on Ninth and Broadway into town to the Center Theater on Main Street in downtown Little Rock. Admission to the movie theater was one whole dime. The Center was actually a dump and we would have to sit in the balcony then, but the Center was one of the few theaters in town that permitted blacks at all. Actually, we thought sitting in the balcony was the best part. We had a better view of the screen and we could look down and laugh at the straight-haired kids below. You could actually get away with throwing popcorn down below as long as you didn't get caught. Years later, Connie and I would go to one of the fancier theaters in the city at the time, sit on the main floor and watch the colorized version of *Gone with the Wind*.

Sunday dinners were always the same – fried chicken, mashed potatoes, green peas and corn bread. During the summer months we would always have a fresh green salad with lettuce, tomatoes and cucumbers from my father's garden. I remember on a few occasions my father treated us to Sunday dinner at one of the soul food diners on Ninth Street, and guess what we ordered – fried chicken, mashed potatoes, green peas and cornbread.

Occasionally, my father would surprise us with a special treat. On our way home from the Sunday evening worship, he might stop at the drug store and we could get ice cream; or if the Krispy Kreme Donut store was still open, we would get donuts. I guess this was our reward for spending all day at church.

Although I am older than television, I don't ever recall not having a television in the home. In the house on Ringo Street we had one of the big old cabinet model TVs in the living room. At that time, a television was considered just as much a piece of furniture as a couch or table. There weren't as many choices as to what to watch and I don't recall too many arguments about what show we would watch. The biggest arguments occurred over whose turn it was to get up and change the channel. Thank God for that much later invention known as the remote control.

Remember the first color TV? Well, it really wasn't color television but a colored plastic sheet you would place over the television screen. Everything at the top of the screen was blue; everything in the middle was an orange/brown or red; and the bottom was green. We had a great time 'pretending'.

Our first portable TV was placed in the 'girls' room'. This portable TV had a handle at the top so that you could carry it from room to room. However, the thing was in a red metal case and weighed about a ton – so much for portable. But the screen was much smaller than the larger TV in the living room.

On Sunday afternoons when we did have a break between the Sunday morning services and the evening services, after we had eaten Sunday dinner and read the comic section of the paper, one of our favorite past-times was to gather around the TV for whatever Sunday specials were on. The Wizard of Oz always came on Sunday afternoon, once a year. However, we were never privileged to see the end because we always had to leave after the first hour to go to ACE League and evening worship service. No matter how hard we cried and protested, it never made any difference. I do believe I was in college before I saw the Wizard of Oz in its' entirety.

Another favorite Sunday afternoon show of mine and Allena's was the (your) *Hit Parade*. There were few, if any Black TV role models at that time. So, when we watched the *Hit Parade*, Allena would pretend to be the blonde singers and I was the brunette singers. Boy did we sing up a storm pretending to be TV singing stars. (One's imagination is a marvelous thing. With all of today's technology, kids don't have to pretend – too bad!)

Christmases

The Christmas season was also a very special time in the R.K. Young household. There was always a huge tree and lots of toys and gifts. Mommy made sure that each one of us got everything we wanted and then some. As I'm sure it was true for every young child, it was difficult to go to sleep on Christmas Eve; and we were always up at the crack of dawn to see what Santa had brought. But in the R.K. Young household you had to wait a little while longer before you could begin ripping open well wrapped presents and playing with new toys. You see, the Reverend always had sunrise service at Bethel on Christmas morning. So instead of running to see what was under the tree, we got up before dawn, got dressed and were off to sunrise service. Here again, you could complain and cry all you wanted, but it made no difference. So, the best thing to do was to just accept it and be happy.

As we would pass through the living room on our way out of the house, we would stretch our necks, looking as hard as we could to see what was under the tree. I guess the long wait made us even more excited when we returned from church and were actually able to open our presents. There were always toys and new clothes.

We each got our individual toys, but every Christmas my Mother (who we knew was the real Santa Claus) would have also bought one- or two-family board games. So, after Christmas morning breakfast and before a scrumptious Christmas dinner, we spent most of the afternoon playing board games – *Monopoly, Clue, Scrabble, Life,* etc. – every year there would be a new game.

When we became older teenagers, my mother would let us do most of our own Christmas shopping so we could get exactly what we wanted, (especially clothes and shoes). However, there would always be a special, secret gift under the tree for each of us. My mother always believed in keeping a little bit of surprise in this holiday.

As a child on most Christmases, after Christmas at our house, we would pile in the car that evening or the following morning and head out on that 4 ½ hour trip to Jackson, Mississippi to my mother's parents' home. There it was Christmas morning all over again – a large tree with lots of gifts for everyone. We always seemed to be entertained on those trips. I don't remember asking too often, "Are we there yet?" Christmases were church, fun, food, and family, usually in that order.

Our New Home

It was in 1958, around the time I turned ten that we moved from the parsonage in Little Rock to our own home in the new housing development for Blacks - Glenview in North Little Rock. Glenview was located in a part of North Little Rock which probably at the time was considered rural. The area had previously been called Tie Plant because there was a large facility there that produced and stored railroad ties. The house in Glenview was my parents dream home; both had input in the design of the house. My mother desperately wanted a house of her own, one that the church did not have control over. And of course, my father had a passion for land and home ownership. By the time we moved to Glenview Emley was already in college, and Rufus was in Jackson, Mississippi with my grandparents. Emley had attended my grandmother's school in Jackson as a young child. She started school at the age of four and had graduated high school by age 15.

When we moved from the house on Ringo Street we did so in phases, making as many trips as necessary over several days taking things to the new house in Glenview. We did not have to worry about moving too much furniture because most of the furniture in the house on Ringo Street belonged to the church. One of the last things to move was the family dog, Spotty. For some reason Daddy claimed not to care too much for Spotty. I never could understand why he was ambivalent toward the dog. Growing up on a farm you would think he would be more compassionate towards animals. At any rate, once we had moved everything else into our home, we returned to Ringo one afternoon to get Spotty. Much to our dismay, Spotty was nowhere in sight. We went up and down the block looking for and calling Spotty's name. When she did not respond we finally left going to our new home feeling a little bit less than complete. When we informed Daddy that we could not find Spotty, he did not seem the least bit concerned. In fact, he seemed somewhat relieved.

About a week later, Mommy, James Robert, Allena and I returned to the Ringo Street house for one final check before turning the keys back over to the church trustees. As we were approaching the house, Phyllis Carter, my best neighborhood friend, came running towards the car hollering that she had found Spotty and had locked her on the small porch on the back of the parsonage. What a reunion – we were all so excited! But our excitement was short lived because we did not know how we were going to break the news to Daddy.

After we left Ringo Street the four of us were driving to pick Daddy up at the church on Ninth and Broadway. Our best bet was to try and hide Spotty so Daddy wouldn't see her until after we got to Glenview. So, James Robert, Allena and I put Spotty on the floor of the back seat and took our coats and covered her. We kept trying to calm Spotty and keep her quiet and still until we got to our new home. However, no more than 5 minutes into our 30 minutes ride home from the church Spotty got antsy and as much as we tried to keep her down, she popped her head from under our coats and let out a loud yelp! Daddy was behind the wheel driving and when Spotty yelped Daddy jerked his head around and a big grin came across his face. Laughing Daddy said, "Where did she come from?" The reunion was complete and all were happy! Daddy was genuinely happy to see Spotty.

Even in the house in North Little Rock there was still the girls' room and the boys' room, but our new home also had a fourth bedroom, which was the guest bedroom and Emley's room when she was home from college. This house was a ranch style home (only one level) that sat on the corner of Glenview Boulevard and Edmonds Street. I did not realize until my father's death that ours' was the largest house in this development.

Yard work became a family affair as well. Mommy loved trees and outdoor plants and flowers. Because it was a new development, most of the trees had been removed for the building of the homes. So, Mommy set out to plant as many trees as possible – all kinds of fruit trees, pecan trees, pine trees, weeping willow – and I remember outside the window of Allena and my bedroom was a mimosa tree. One time on a trip to Atlanta to visit Emley, my mother had my father pull over on the side of the highway so that she and James Robert could dig up some small pine trees to plant in her yard.

Mommy planted and it was James Robert, Allena and I who had to do all the weeding of the flower garden and the shrubbery. I think that is why to this day I detest yard work. I'd rather pay someone to take care of the yard.

Mommy planted trees, shrubbery and flowers; and Daddy planted his garden of vegetables – corn, tomatoes, cucumbers, green peppers, squash, potatoes – you name it. Daddy would share the bounty of his garden with neighbors, friends and family. However, others would take advantage of the harvest themselves. One morning we found a salt shaker amongst the rows of tomatoes. I guess someone had come prepared and when they heard noise in the house, took off and dropped their salt shaker.

We lived next door to the principal of the elementary school which was right across the street from our house. The school sat on the corner of Edmonds Street and East 19th Street. My mother transferred to the North Little Rock school system and after two years, at her request, she was transferred to that school. At the time it was called Roosevelt Elementary School. The name was later changed to Glenview Elementary School. Since we moved midway through the school year, James Robert, Allena and I completed that school year in the Little Rock system. I only attended Roosevelt for my sixth-grade year. And then it was on to Junior High School (no such thing as middle school back in those days).

High School Days

No matter your socio-economic status or where you lived in North Little Rock – if you were Black, you attended Scipio Africanus Jones Junior and Senior High School. Although there were several elementary schools for Blacks in North Little Rock, there was only one high school. From grades seven through twelve it was Dear Ole Jones. It was a while before I knew who Scipio Africanus Jones was. From the picture of him that hung on the wall outside of the main office in the school, I originally thought our school was named after a white man, which would not have been unusual for those times. Later I was to learn that Scipio Africanus Jones (1863-1943) was an African American educator, attorney, judge, philanthropist, and Republican politician there in Arkansas. He was most noted for his role in defending twelve black men sentenced to death following the Elaine (Phillips County, AR) Massacre of 1919, in which hundreds of blacks were killed by whites in a labor dispute. The black sharecroppers, who had formed a group known as the Progressive Farmers and Household Union, were demanding more for their crops. And although many more blacks were killed in this massacre than whites (it is reported that only 5 whites were killed); it was the blacks who were brought to trial for killing white men. *(The Encyclopedia of Arkansas History and Culture - http://www.encyclopediaofarkansas. net/encyclopedia/entry-detail.aspx?entryID=2427).*

Scipio Africanus Jones was also a member and trustee at Bethel AME Church. He is buried at the *Haven of Rest Cemetery*, which is the largest African American cemetery in the state of Arkansas. Many other notable blacks in Arkansas history are buried in the Haven of Rest Cemetery, including Joseph Albert Booker (1859–1926), noted editor, educator, and community leader, who for four decades was a prominent leader in Arkansas racial relations and a pioneer in African-American education in the state. It is also the final earthly resting place for Rev. Rufus King Young, Sr.

When I started seventh grade, James Robert was in the ninth grade. He was a star football player and a great talker. So, everyone knew 'Tank' as he was called; and I was just Tank's little sister. I don't know when I developed into a timid and shy person, but I recall being that way during most of my junior high and senior high school days. I always had friends and folks I could talk to – if I wanted to, but I just didn't feel the need to be all that sociable. I guess it was just a period in my life. At heart though, I do consider myself an introvert – the quiet one, the one who is completely content being alone. Even today I treasure my time alone. (Odd that

I would marry a man who is the complete opposite and will talk to anybody.) I believe most of us suffer from a multiple personality disorder and can turn on the personality we need for the particular situation. But don't get me wrong – I did enjoy my high school days. I was the good one; the teachers' pet. My senior year, I was voted by the faculty and staff at Jones as *Best Citizen* – that was me.

When James Robert, Allena and I talk about those days at Jones I sometimes wonder how we made it through. I can remember a shooting in the hallway during lunch time. I can remember when Mr. Beavers, the boys' counselor, performed a locker search to confiscate all illegal items. When I visited Mr. Beavers' office after one such locker check it looked like an arsenal – guns, chains, knifes and all other kinds of unknown paraphernalia.

I also remember sitting in front of the school waiting on my father to pick me up after school one day when a loud gang formed around two young men who were fighting. I did not know if they were students at Jones or not. But there, right in front of me I saw one of the young men severely cut the other with a knife – blood everywhere. Now these were not everyday occurrences, but they did happen. None of these incidents ever made the 6:00 o'clock news because the truth of the matter is that during those times, they would not have even been considered newsworthy. The funny thing is I never felt afraid or in danger. There seemed to be some unwritten code; and even the worst of the so-called *thugs* seemed to be protective of the good ones – oh, and did I already say I was one of the good ones.

There were train tracks that ran behind the school, several rows of tracks. The only thing that separated the school from the train tracks was an old wire fence. The train tracks separated Jones High from one of the Black areas of North Little Rock, which at the time was referred to as Dark Hollow. Over the years, students had made several passageways by cutting or pulling back loose wire from the fence. It was repeatedly announced for students not to cross the train tracks, but to go down to the cross over or the viaduct. This warning was constantly ignored because students would have to walk what seemed like a mile out of the way just to get to the cross over bridge. It saved a great deal of time just to cut through one of the openings in the fence and race across the tracks. At least once a year a student or someone was killed racing across those tracks.

Jones High School with all its faults was truly a learning ground that prepared you for life. All of the teachers cared and tried to do their best with what they had. They knew all of their students by name and in most cases knew their families. My sixth-grade principal and teacher, my high school principal and many of the high school teachers lived in the Glenview subdivision. I don't recall there every being any class distinction – we were all just young black kids trying to make it. I don't even recall asking anyone – what does your mother or father do? It really didn't matter and I don't think anyone much cared. However, I think most everyone knew my mother was a teacher because she taught many of their younger siblings, and that my father was Rev. Young.

The Jones High mascot was a dragon; and I think due to a collaborative effort between the Art and the Vocational Departments, a huge dragon made out of wood, wire netting and paper-mâché and colored green and brown was erected. I don't know how tall this thing was, but during my high school days I could swear it was about eight feet tall. This mascot stood in the center of the hallway in front of the gym/auditorium; and was the first thing you saw when you entered the front doors of Jones. I don't know how long it had been there, but it was there when I entered Jones in the seventh grade.

Dear Ole Jones
Our hearts for you are tender;
Dear Ole Jones
Your love we will remember;
The days of work and pleasure
Are moments we will treasure
As we go out from here on our way.

Excerpts from S.A. Jones High School Alma Mater
(Lyrics by Virginia R. Robinson and arranged by Juanita
S. Thompson, both of whom were my teachers.)

Jones doesn't exist anymore. The North Little Rock School system was integrated in 1968/69 and Jones High School was closed in 1970. The building no longer exists; it was destroyed in 1973. The only structure remaining is the Health and Physical Education building, which was constructed in 1968, after I graduated. Any artifacts remaining have been preserved and are housed at the National Alumni Association building on Pine Street in North Little Rock.

Getting from Here to There

Because we were a family of seven, my parents always drove a large car. Of course, this was well before the days of Minivans and six or seven passenger SUVs. During my growing-up days it was the family station wagon. During the early days, my parents owned only one car. My mother was only able to use the car when my father was not about church business, which was rare. I don't quite remember when we became a two-car family.

I also don't remember all of the different cars my family owned when I was growing up. But the one car I will never forget, and perhaps the most notable of all cars, was a three-tone pink Desoto station wagon. I remember the day my Dad came home with this monstrosity. James Robert, Allena and I stood looking at the thing not knowing whether to laugh or cry. I can only imagine that my Dad must have gotten a real good deal on it because no one else would touch it.

I can remember being very embarrassed to ride in the very bright, "can't help but be seen" car, especially when my father would drop me off or pick me up from school. But I can also remember being very happy to ride in that three-tone pink monstrosity as opposed to riding the public bus, which in the 60s in Arkansas still presented a challenge for many Black commuters. There were no Black bus drivers during that time, and even if you were standing right next to the bus stop sign, the white drivers would stop the bus directly in front of the white passengers. Sometimes we would literally have to push and shove just to get on the bus, and sometime fight to get a seat.

In addition, I was a senior in high school before the North Little Rock Public School system decided to provide school bus services for the Black students in the Tie Plant/Glenview area to get to Jones Junior and Senior High School. Prior to that, there was only one city bus that came to our area in the morning and again in late afternoon. The bus took you to downtown North Little Rock. From there you had to transfer to another bus to get to your final destination.

Little Rock and the Civil Rights Movement

March on Washington – Little Rock NAACP Delegation
Back of Rev. Young as he leads prayer

I was only eight years old in 1957 when those nine brave students integrated Central High School in Little Rock, Arkansas. So, at my age I did not realize the historical significance of what was going on at the time. Most of my memories are the impact these times had on my mother. We were still living in the house on Ringo Street. Emley has the greatest memories of these days because Ernest Green, the oldest of the Little Rock Nine was her classmate at Horace Mann High School, the Black High School. Actually, Emley had the opportunity to be a part of the students to integrate Central High. She actually attended the orientation meetings. However, as she puts it, "it was my senior year and I did not want to miss out on all of the fun and activities that your senior year in high school brings, especially the senior prom." So, she decided not to participate. With this decision my mother sighed a sigh of relief (remember Mommy was the cautious one). My father on the other hand, although he never said so, may have been a little bit disappointed (remember Daddy was the brave one).

But Rev. Young took a very active role in this struggle. He was one of the key negotiators who initiated and activated the plan to desegregate Central High School. Three of the Little Rock Nine were members of my father's church: Ernest Green, Melba Pattillo and Gloria Ray; and Carlotta Walls had attended Bethel at times with relatives. (Melba Pattillo's mother would later be my 10th grade English teacher at Jones High School.) Also, Daisy Bates, who was the advisor to the Nine and Atty. Christopher Mercer, who was field secretary for the NAACP and assigned to Mrs. Bates and the Nine were members of Bethel during my father's pastorate.

At the time of the integration of Central High School, Bethel AME Church was situated at the corner of Ninth and Broadway. My Father was one of the few pastors who allowed organizational meetings to be held at his church. Even against the protest of some of the members, he felt it was his responsibility to help guide and protect. In an interview for the *Arkansas Gazette* at the time of his retirement in 1986, of those times Daddy said, "I saw my role as giving moral and spiritual undergirding to the civil rights movement and to those students who were under such severe pressure... As (the Old Testament book) Daniel was written to give courage to the Jews under persecution and Revelation was written to encourage

Christians who were suffering, I endeavored to fulfill such a prophetic role – to give strength to persevere in the present age and to instill the hope God was going to take care of this situation."

My mother and father were to have attended Ernest Green's graduation from Central High School. However, because of the tense climate in Little Rock at the time, my mother (being the cautious one) chose not to go. My father was determined that he would attend, and as he put it, Emley was not afraid of anything, so he and Emley attended Ernest Green's graduation ceremony, the first black in history to graduate from Central High School. Emley says you could feel the tension in the air, but here again, she was not afraid because she was with my father. Of course, there were only a few blacks in attendance, but Emley remembers sitting only a few seats away from Dr. Martin Luther King, Jr.

It was during these tumultuous times that the Rev. Rufus King Young, Sr. was elected president of the integrated ministerial alliance, the first black minister to hold that position. In the 2001 Documentary, *We Shall Not Be Moved,* Henry McHenry, who was the first African American to serve as Arkansas' Director of Employment Security under Governors Dale Bumpers, David Pryor and Bill Clinton states, "Rev. Young felt he owed no allegiance to anyone except God, his church and his members. So, he was not about to get on any side of an issue except what he considered to be the right side. So, supporting the Little Rock Nine; supporting Daisy Bates; supporting her husband, L. C. Bates was the right thing to do – and he did it."

We Shall Overcome became the theme song of the Civil Rights movement of the sixties. One of the verses of that song says *God is on our side.* Of those times, my father would recall being interviewed by a reporter who made a statement and then asked the question – You sing that you shall overcome and that God is on your side. How do you know that God is on your side? To which Rev. Young replied, "I don't worry too much about God being on my side. I just want to make sure that I am on God's side". And he knew that he was.

Although Daisy Bates changed her membership from Bethel to worship with her husband, L. C. Bates, Rev. Young remained one of her spiritual advisors and friends. Daisy Bates died in November, 1999. She too is buried in the historic Haven of Rest Cemetery. On the occasion of her memorial service which was held in April 2000, with the Governor of Arkansas, Mike Huckabee and President William Clinton present, my father provided the following remarks, which sums up how they survived the hatred and inhumanity of those times. *(Printed in its entirety.)*

To the Chairman of the Bates Memorial Committee, Mr. Larry Ross, Mayor Jim Dailey, Governor Mike Huckabee, and Mr. President William Jefferson Clinton – GREETINGS.

First of all, Mr. President I want to say how glad we are to see you here today all in one piece. For the way hell hounds have been viciously yelping on your tracks for the past eight or ten months, we felt sure by now they would have caught you and torn you all to pieces. But we believe that one of the reasons they have not been able to do this is because so many black folks have been praying for you. Black folks like Daisy Bates.

So then, allow me if you please, to put the words of David into the mouth of Daisy Bates and have her speak them as though they were her own. The words are recorded in the 23rd number of Psalms at the 4th verse, as in the King James Version reads thusly, "Though I walk through the valley of the shadow of death, I will fear no evil, for thou art with me, thy rod and thy staff they comfort me."

"LIVING UNDER THE SHADOW OF DEATH"

In a very real sense, we all live under the shadow of death. From the day we are born until the day we die; from the cradle to the grave; from the basket to the casket; from the womb to the tomb; from the time we are conceived in our mothers' womb until the time we are received into the womb of mother earth. This being true, the question arises Miss Daisy, how can you live successfully under the Shadow of Death?

"Well, I tell you Rufus in order to do this, the first thing you have to do is get rid of fear. Gideon started out with 32 thousand men to fight the Midianites. God told him he had too many. In order to thin them down the first test was the fear test. All who were afraid were asked to go home. Twenty-two thousand went home. You see, fear paralyzes, fear deactivates, fear debilitates, fear immobilizes, fear degenerates."

Yes, but I tell you Miss Daisy, before you take off too hastily down that road you better look down it to see what's there. Look down, look down that lonesome road before you travel it alone.

"Well, you see Rufus, I have already done that."

You have Miss Daisy? What did you see?

"Well I saw the Long Shadow of Little Rock stretching across my way and out of that shadow emerged the Ku Klux Klan burning a cross on my lawn; racists breaking the picture window of my home; the police, who instead of arresting those who vandalized my home, arrested my neighbor who volunteered to protect my home. I see economic boycotters that caused me to become unable to pay the notes on my home and threatened with foreclosure; political enemies who passed laws designed to put the NAACP out of business, requiring it to turn over its membership rolls; and school teachers having to sign affidavits stating that they were not members of the NAACP before they were issued a contract; Commercializers seeking to cash in on you whatever way they can. But I still say, "I will fear no evil."

But Miss Daisy, you had better take a second look down the road before you go ahead.

"I have."

Well, what did you see?

"I saw lurking in the historical crevices of that road, the Bull of Bashan, the Beast of Ephesus, the Ephraim backsliding Heifer, Leviathan, the Apocalyptic Dragon of the Seven Seas; and old Lucifer the Devil himself. But I still say, "I will fear no evil." You see one of the Little Rock Nine, Melba Pattillo Beals, whom I pastored, wrote a book entitled, "Warriors Don't Cry", Warriors don't cry, they fight!!! "Sure, I must fight if I would reign, increase my courage, Lord, I'll bear the toil, endure the pain, supported by Thy Word."

Well now, Miss Daisy, "How do you get rid of fear?"

"Well now to do this you must get somebody to walk with you who is able to take care of whatever situation that may arise along the way. Thou art with me!"

Well now Miss Daisy, who is this "Thou" you have so much confidence in?

"Well he is known by different names by different people, in different places. The writer of that first creation story in the first chapter of Genesis called him Elohim, translated – God. The man who wrote the second creation in the second chapter of Genesis called him Yahweh Elohim, translated Lord God of Jehovah God. Abraham called him El Shaddai – God Almighty; David called him the Ancient of Days; Moses called him I Am, that I am – He that was, and is, and will forever be. Daniel called him the Ancient of Days – one who antecedes days and nights. David called him Shepherd – therefore he did not have to want for anything. Jesus called him Father, and taught us to say when we pray – "Our Father", thereby laying the foundation for worldwide brotherhood and sisterhood.

John the Revelation called him Alpha and Omega, the first and the last, the beginning and the end. Zoroaster called him Ahure Mazda. The Hindus called him The World Soul, the source of all souls and to which they will return. Confucius called him Heaven. Muhammad called him Allah. For Buddha, He breaks through language and escapes to the domain of the un-nameable. The Scientist called him the first cause or the Prime Mover. He is the cause behind all causes and he made the move that started everything; the move to moving.

But by whatever name, His functions are the same. He is bread in a starving land and water in dry places;
He is a rock in a weary land and a shelter in the time of storm;
He is a bridge over deep waters, a mighty fortress and a high tower;
He is a mother for the motherless and a father for the fatherless;
He is a husband for the widows and a friend for the friendless;
He locks the lion's jaw and fans all the heat out of the fire;
He sets the captives free and liberates those who are in bondage;
He lifts up the fallen and makes somebodies out of nobodies;
He descends from wherever He is way up there, to wherever you are way down here;
And He takes care of whatever situation you are in.
"He walks with me and He talks with me and He tells me I am His own."

So now I see Miss Daisy, you have agility in your footsteps, and instancey (immediacy) in your pace. You are half way strutting now. So, strut in all the dignity of your black liberated femininity. Strut in all the blessed assurance of your divine security. You are strutting like you have seen light at the end of the tunnel called the "Shadow of Death", and you see standing there to greet you, your companion in tribulation, L.C. Bates, Martin Luther King, Jr., John Fitzgerald Kennedy, Robert Kennedy, and the angel Gabriel with a pair of wings for you. Now you know "Why the Caged Bird Sings," because we know he has wings. And, just as soon as you get out of this cage called "The Shadow of Death", you are going to hitch on your wings and try the air. You are going to take a little eschatological flight to the domain of the Eschaton, there to dwell forever, where there will be no more sorrow, sickness, pain or death. AMEN, HALLELUJAH, PRAISE THE LORD!!!

Daddy took on every fight for justice and equality. In 1963, Rev. Young was one of the leaders in organizing the delegation from Little Rock that would travel by bus to the Nation's Capital to participate in the historic March on Washington for jobs and freedom. With estimated crowds of between 200,000 and 300,000 Dr. Martin Luther King, Jr. delivered his "I Have a Dream" speech. In 1965, Rev. Young was among the 25,000 who assembled in Montgomery, Alabama at the steps of the State Capitol building to see Governor George Wallace in support of voting rights. It was here that Dr. King, Jr. delivered another one his many famous speeches, "How Long, Not Long." This occurred just 18 days after *"Bloody Monday"* on the Edmund Pettis Bridge as the first group of protesters unsuccessfully attempted to march from Selma to Montgomery.

Rev. Young never backed down when he felt he was in the right, and when he knew he needed to take a stand. He spoke his mind. Recently I heard a young minister say when God gives you something to say, you can't hold your tongue. That was Daddy – And he did have something to say.

The New Church –
The New Bethel

By the mid-fifties Broadway Street, as it is today, was a major thoroughfare in Little Rock. Ninth Street, up until you reached Broadway was populated with black owned and/or operated businesses – barbershops, beauty parlors, eateries, liquor stores, night clubs, etc. Once you crossed over Broadway, Bethel was the only thing remaining of the black community. The church was surrounded by gas stations, car dealerships, auto repair shops and office buildings. That corner became increasingly more dangerous, especially for children on Sunday mornings and activities during the week. Even though we were told not to, every Sunday we would slip across the street to the gas station to buy treats from the *Lance* vending machines that were located outside near the gas pumps.

Parking near the church was also becoming a problem. The church was also in much disrepair. The lower basement of the church contained a fellowship hall, where Sunday School and ACE League were conducted. There were classrooms on either side of the fellowship/auditorium area; there was a stage with a classroom on either side of the stage; and a dining area and the kitchen. The Pastor's study and the church secretary's office were also located in this lower area.

I don't know if it was because it was located underground, but the basement area always appeared to be damp and dank. In the summer months due to condensation, there would actually be puddles of water on the basement floor. In the winter, you didn't know how to dress for the basement; it was either too cold or those old radiators were really working and you burnt up. In the winter there would also be puddles of water from the steam from the radiators. We often complained that our Sunday hairdos, with our curls and bangs, would quickly become frizzy from the humidity in the basement.

Old Bethel A.M.E. Church (Ninth and Broadway)
Lower Auditorium Dining Hall
Far Rear: Rev. and Mrs. Young, Ellen, Allena, and
(over one) James Robert

The sanctuary was upstairs and to me it appeared to be enormous (once again, things always appear to be larger to a child). I'm sure the sanctuary in its heyday had been a spectacular sight. Next door to the church, there sat a house on the same lot and built from the same brick. This house had once been the church parsonage, but at the time we came to Bethel it was used for the beginners and primary Sunday School classes. This area was no longer considered residential. The cathedral style structure on Ninth and Broadway was originally built in 1871, which was the second structure on this site. Between 1923 and 1925 the third church underwent an extensive remodeling and renovation. But because of the lack of proper upkeep, by the late 1950s, the structure was literally falling apart. A severe storm came through Little Rock and actually caused part of the ceiling in the sanctuary to fall. It was actually unsafe for us to even enter the building.

It was in 1958 that the church purchased the whole block of land on 16th Street between South Izard and South State streets. The decision to build a new church and not to try and repair the property on Ninth and Broadway did not come without controversy and dissention. There was a contingency of the membership who vigorously protested the sale of the Ninth street property. I can remember my father coming home from some of those heated meetings looking and feeling very forlorn. I know he prayed long and hard over this matter. Daddy later admitted that this was perhaps the most difficult time of his ministry.

The groundbreaking for the new church at 815 West 16th Street took place in 1963. The Christian Education wing was to be constructed first. It was that same year that Daddy and a congregation of adults and youth boarded a bus in Little Rock and headed to the historic March on Washington. I was 14 at the time and remember watching the coverage of the March on television and trying to see if I could see my father in that massive crowd.

The Bethel congregation was displaced for approximately two years during the construction of the Christian Education facility. During that time, they worshipped in the former Emmanuel Baptist Church building on Chester Street. This was actually an unfinished facility, just one level area. My recollection was that this building was just as damp and dank as the basement of the Ninth and Broadway facility.

The Christian Education building of the New Bethel was

completed in 1966 and the first Worship Service was conducted in the Fellowship Hall in February of that year. The sanctuary was completed in 1970.

Isn't it interesting that the first wedding to be performed in the new sanctuary was that of Rev. R.K. Young's middle daughters – that would be me! I was married in the brand-new structure on August 22, 1970, two months after it was completed. All members, including those who opposed the sale of the Ninth Street property were excited to be in their new church home.

There was even more excitement when only nine years after the completion of the sanctuary; thirteen years after occupying the Christian Education building; and twenty-one years after the purchase of the property, the entire mortgage and all other costs associated with the relocation were *paid in full*. The church celebrated with a mortgage burning ceremony.

Today, Bethel AME Church still sits on that block of land on 16th Street in Little Rock. The library, which is part of the Christian Education facility was expanded and a work space addition was completed in 1983. Other improvements were made to the church facility in 2002; and more recently a media system was installed. There have been eight senior pastors at Bethel since Rev. Young's retirement in 1986.

In 2013, Bethel celebrated its' 150th anniversary. In the 150-year history of the church there have been a total of 28 different pastors of Bethel (six pastors served two different time period). To date, Rev. Rufus King Young, Sr. still holds the record for the longest serving pastor of this historic institution which has served as a beacon to the Little Rock community and the State of Arkansas. (*Most information on church history obtained from the 150th Anniversary Program Booklet.*)

**New Bethel – Corner Stone Laying Ceremony
for Sanctuary - 1970**
Center: Essie Mae Young, Rufus K. Young

**Rev. and Mrs. R.K. Young and Three Youngest
Children in the Pastor's Office of New Bethel**
Left to Right: James Robert, Mrs. Young, Ellen, Allena
Seated: Rev. Young

49

The Bishopric

Rev. Rufus King Young, Sr., although not born into the AME Church, was devoted to his denomination. For those who are not familiar with African Methodism, the African Methodist Episcopal Church has a rich and unique history as it is the first major religious denomination in the western world that developed because of sociological rather than theological differences. It was the first African-American denomination organized and incorporated in the United States. The church was born in protest against racial discrimination in of all places, houses of worship. *(https://www. ame-church.com/)*

According to the African Methodist Episcopal Church official website:

> The AME Church grew out of the Free African Society (FAS) which Richard Allen, Absalom Jones, and others established in Philadelphia in 1787. When officials at St. George's Methodist Episcopal Church pulled blacks off their knees while praying, FAS members discovered just how far American Methodists would go to enforce racial discrimination against African Americans. Hence, these members of St. George's made plans to transform their mutual aid society into an African congregation. Although most wanted to affiliate

with the Protestant Episcopal Church, Allen led a small group who resolved to remain Methodists. In 1794 Bethel AME was dedicated with Allen as pastor. To establish Bethel's independence from interfering white Methodists, Allen, a former Delaware slave, successfully sued in the Pennsylvania courts in 1807 and 1815 for the right of his congregation to exist as an independent institution. Allen was consecrated its first bishop in 1816. (Dennis C. Dickerson, "Our History," on the African Methodist Episcopal Church website, https://www.ame-church.com/our-church/our-history/, accessed August 7, 2020)

Today, the African Methodist Episcopal Church has membership in twenty Episcopal Districts in thirty-nine countries on five continents. The work of the Church is administered by twenty-one active bishops, and nine General Officers who manage the departments of the Church.

The highest rank in the African Methodist Episcopal Church is that of *Bishop*. AME Bishops are the Chief Officers of the Connectional Organization. They are elected by a majority vote of the General Conference which meets every four years. There is a bishop assigned to each of the Episcopal Districts of the AME Church. (Today there are 20 Episcopal Districts.) My father sought this highest office in the church on three separate occasions; the General Conferences in 1960, 1972 and 1976. Each loss brought about new disappointments for Daddy for he genuinely believed that he had something to offer the AME Church at that level. He believed he could institute the changes he felt were necessary for the church denomination.

His last run for the Episcopacy was at the General Conference held in Atlanta, Georgia in 1976. I watched this quest for the highest office in the AME Church almost kill my father. His campaign was truly a family affair. Emley and Rufus, Jr., who were living in

Atlanta at that time; and the other three Younguns, as well as all spouses and grandchildren at the time were there. Between Emley's home and Rufus, Jr.'s home we had a production line going on. We were assembling gift baskets for the current sitting Bishops, and preparing and sorting campaign materials. It was not until I was directly involved in the process that I saw what it could do to one physically, mentally and spiritually. I guess I would have expected such goings-on in a political campaign, but not in the church. It was truly an eye-opener.

One afternoon as we had completed one of our campaign tasks at Rufus, Jr.'s home, we were all headed to our cars to return to the convention center. As Daddy reached the car (passenger's side) I saw his body slump and he was headed for the ground. I remember screaming – I imagine my sisters were screaming as well. I don't know who caught Daddy before he hit the ground – Rufus Jr. or James Robert, but Daddy had to be rushed to the hospital. He was diagnosed with a bleeding ulcer. He was sixty-five years old at the time and Mommy said that was it – she had spoken.

Retirement

Daddy continued in the pulpit at Bethel until the mandatory retirement age in the AME Church of 75. He retired amidst great fanfare and festivities. A large retirement banquet was held for him at the Robinson Auditorium in Little Rock. Ministers from all over the Twelfth Episcopal District were in attendance. The Presiding Prelate of the 12th District at the time, Bishop H. Hartford Brookins was the keynote speaker for the occasion. Those providing tributes included Rodney Slater, who was then the Executive Assistant to the Governor of Arkansas and later became the U.S. Secretary of Transportation under the Clinton administration.

Daddy's retirement was acknowledged by numerous other bishops who had served the 12th district; general officers of the AME Church; Bill Clinton, who was then the Governor of Arkansas; as well as other state officials and religious leaders. Of course, all of the five Younguns, their spouses and children were present for this momentous occasion. I regret that Mommy could not have lived to see that day and enjoy retirement with the Reverend.

At the time of his retirement, Daddy had the following reflections:

> Standing at the end of my pastoral journey in the Christian Ministry, reflecting upon the many experiences I've had along the way, I am overwhelmed with a deep sense of indebtedness

that I owe to all of the loving, kind and generously helpful people that it has been my fortune to meet along the way. I am truly thankful to God who deemed me worthy to be called to this Ministry. I am grateful to Him, who through his Son Jesus Christ, saved me and sent me on my way with the assuring promise that He would be with me...

I want to say to all the Bishops, Presiding Elders, Pastors, Officers, Members and Friends with whom I have served along the way – THANKS A MILLION – for all that you have said or done to help along the way. Special thanks to the Beloved Officers and Members and Friends of the Bethel Family with whom I spent more than half of those sixty-two years of service. You will never know how much my serving you has meant to me for the past thirty-three years. It is my fervent prayer that God in his eternal goodness will ever bless each of you all along life's tedious and uneven journey. AMEN! *(RKY, Sr.)*

Daddy's Retirement - 1986
Top Left to Right: James Robert, Daddy, Rufus, Jr.
Bottom Left to Right: Daddy, Allena, Ellen, Emley

He may have retired from the pulpit, but he did not retire from the AME Church or working for the betterment of people of color. He continued to be very active on all levels of the AME Church and continued his membership at Bethel AME Church, Little Rock until his death at the age of ninety-three in 2004.

A great tribute was paid to him in 2002, when Rev. Rickey H. Hicks, Pastor of Connor Chapel AME Church located at 2100 Main Street in Little Rock and its members voted to change the name of their church to the ***Rufus Young AME Church***, in honor of Rev. Young's sixty-two years in the ministry and his practice of standing up for what was right in the community. The church is still on Main Street in Little Rock, but is now known as the Rufus Young Christian Church.

Also, after his retirement, the Greater Little Rock Christian Ministerial Alliance honored him with an annual humanitarian award named after him – the Dr. R. K. Young Humanitarian Award. This Ministerial Alliance, with my father at the forefront, was instrumental in getting Daisy Bates' home designated as a National Historic Landmark and raising the funds to restore the home.

On the occasion of this ninetieth birthday in 2001, many of those who grew up at Bethel under the pastorate of Rev. Young held a ninetieth birthday party for him at the church. All of them now were calling themselves the *Younguns*, for they all gave Rev. Young credit for helping to shape and mold their lives. It was on this occasion that the following tribute was given to him by his children.

OH! WHAT A MAN!

Humble, mild-mannered, a man whose words are few
Yet, animated, outspoken, sometimes argumentative, too!

Thoughtful, considerate, and respected by everyone
Always toiling, never ceasing 'til his work is done.

When I was a child, I thought he was a giant – a Superman!
But as I grew older, I began to realize that he was just a man.

A man with passion for justice, equality, and what is right.
A man who not only talks the talk, but who's willing to stand up and fight.

A man of the cloth, who has been ordained by God.
Who lives his life by faith, and not by the might of the rod.

If you ask me why so many love and trust him – and from no one
he hides,
Simple, God made him special, and in him joy abides.

Yes, he is just a man – But, oh what a man is he.
Gentle! Caring! Brave! Strong! – Sounds like Superman to me!

Our Dad is super – that's why we love him so.
And today as we celebrate his birth – we just want to let him know.

That no matter how old we get, and where we go in life,
Like the Savior, he has been our anchor, our solace in the midst of
strife.

He is just a man – But, oh what a man is he.
May God continue to bless him throughout all eternity.

Written by eavyf

Mommy

Mommy
Essie Mae Adams Young

A story about R. K. Young and the Young family would not be complete without tribute being paid to the matriarch of the family. R. K. Young and Essie Mae Adams Young were married for over forty-one years at the time of her death and raised five children together.

Essie Mae Adams Young was born October 8, 1920 in Holcomb, MS, which is in Grenada County – about 120 miles north of Jackson. Essie was a devoted daughter, wife, mother and educator. She received her undergraduate degree from Tougaloo College in Tougaloo, MS; and her Master's Degree from University of Arkansas, Fayetteville in 1959. She spent an illustrious career as a public-school teacher. As my father traveled around as an Itinerate Elder in the AME Church, so did my mother's teaching career. She taught at Campbell College in Jackson, MS; Daniel Payne College in Birmingham, AL; and in the public-school systems in Baton Rouge, LA and Prattville, AL.

After moving to Little Rock in 1953, my mother taught in the Pulaski County, the Little Rock and the North Little Rock Public School Systems. Due to her failing health, she retired from the teaching profession in 1980, less than three years prior to her death on February 26, 1983.

Mommy took her role as the Pastor's wife – the first lady - very seriously. Her local church life was very active. In addition to singing in the church choir, she was a class leader, and the intermediate girls Sunday School teacher. She worked in the ACE League and Vacation Bible School; was director and musician for the Children's Choir; and a member of the Bethel's Women's Missionary Society (later named in her honor).

My mother served in various capacities in the Women's Missionary Society at the local, branch, district and connectional levels of the AME church. She was also a much sought-after speaker in the 12ᵗʰ Episcopal District. She was often invited by other churches as their Women's Day or Missionary Day speaker. I would be in awe as I watched my mother speak, for she did it so effortlessly. She had also inherited a little bit of her mother's dramatics. She captured your attention from the beginning and never let you go.

My mother's father was James Lee Adams, who was a trustee in the church and pretty much ran things at Hairs Tabernacle AME Church in Jackson, Mississippi. We called my grandfather "Big Daddy." Big Daddy held a very prominent status in the Black community at that time. In addition to his standing in the church, he was also one of the first Black letter carriers in Jackson. He was also a Notary Public. Both of these were big deals for a black man in Mississippi during the early and middle part of the twentieth century. My mother's mother was Edna Elizabeth Moore. She was the church musician, Sunday School Teacher, church playwright and one of the best cooks in Jackson. She could bake a pie out of just about anything. One time when she was visiting us in Little Rock, she was searching for something to bake a pie. When she realized that we did not have any apples, peaches or the usual stuff that pies are made of, she noticed a large bin of tomatoes. I'd never had a tomato pie before, but believe it or not, it was delicious.

My mother's mother, Big Mother, as we called her, ran a private school for Blacks in their home in Jackson. The back part of the house was specially built for the school, with two or three classrooms and a large eating area, which could also be used as a small auditorium.

My grandparent's home seemed like a mansion to me as a small child. The large house had a wraparound screened in porch. If you were standing facing the house, the porch ran from the front of the house and all the way around the left side of the house. At the left corner of the house there was a closed in office area. This is where Big Daddy would receive his customers who came to get documents notarized. The screened porch would then continue after the office area. We spent most Christmases and every summer with my grandparents in Jackson.

During the summer months, we spent most of the day at the public pool for *Negroes*. Big Daddy would take us in the morning when he went on his route and pick us up in the afternoon on his way home. It's amazing how much time we spent in the water and to this day I do not know how to swim – amazing. I remember many warm summer nights after much begging and pleading with Big Mother, we were allowed to sleep on the screened in porch on the side of the house.

Another fun event of the summer was when the "Mosquito Man" came. Jackson and I suppose all of Mississippi had a big mosquito problem at that time. So at least once every 30 days a large truck would come through the community spraying insecticide. The spray would create a dense fog which you could not even see through. When news spread that the Mosquito Man was coming, all the children would run outside and play and jump up and down in the dense fog. Little did we know that the fumes that were being sprayed and that we were inhaling were hazardous to our health. But no one thought about those things at that time. As an adult I often wondered if the Mosquito Man only sprayed those hazardous fumes in the black communities; and why weren't we ever warned of the potential danger.

My mother was an only child up until she was in her forties. Her father, Big Daddy remarried after Big Mother died in 1959, and he had a son younger than his grandchildren. We lost touch with James Lee Jr. after my mother and grandfather died (both in 1983) and James Jr. and his mother moved to the west coast.

Mommy died due to end organ damage related to diabetes. She went into a diabetic coma shortly after having a leg amputated in November, 1982. She never regained consciousness and remained in the coma for three months.

Tribute to Mommy

As stated, it would be impossible to write anything about my family without paying tribute to my mother, Essie Mae Adams Young. I was only thirty-four years old when my mother went home to be with her Lord. I remember both of my grandmothers quite well. Even though I was only eleven when Big Mother died. I had spent so much of my childhood with her and she was such a character that I have memories to last for two or three lifetimes. I was grown and had two children of my own when my father's mother died in 1978, just a little over a month after my youngest child was born. So, I have fond memories of both grandmothers. One of my biggest regrets is that my girls did not get to know my mother that well. They were only seven and four at the time of my mother's death.

Over the years I have put a lot of thoughts about my mother on paper; and I thought the best way to pay tribute to her is to share some of those writings. Here are a few.

Confession and Prayer
(Written shortly after my mother's death...)

There have been times in my life when I have questioned the existence of God, as I am sure all of us have at sometimes. However, for the past several years I have been closer to God than any other being, human or spiritual.

Yet, with the passing of a loved one, particularly one such as my mother, I did pause for a moment to ask God – WHY?

A woman who knew no other way of existence but to serve and praise your Holy Name;

A woman who was loved by young and old – who touched the life of every person with whom she came in contact;

A Mother, Wife, Friend, Confidant, Counselor, Comforter, Helper, a Christian Woman.

Why, Lord? Why was she taken from me?

However, a moment later I realized - What a selfish thought. Not only was she taken from me, but the rest of the world who knew and loved her.

Do we really mourn the death of our loved ones – or are we agonizing over a personal loss – an inconvenience to our life?

Are we more concerned with how the absence of that person will somehow affect, or possibly change our own life?

Did I really wish for her to continue in her pain and suffering?

Is not her soul at peace and rest with you, O LORD?

She was born,

She lived,

She loved and was loved, and

She died

And most people would say, "That's life". But her life is not over – it has just begun.

For You walked with her each day of her mortal life and now, she walks with You.

Her journey on earth was over and You said – "COME HOME"

Not a day goes by without some thoughts of my mother,
And again, I say – How much more must I suffer?
But Lord, you know just how much we can bear.
I will miss her, God
And I will remember her,
And I will always love her,
But most of all I pray that Thou will continue to guide and
strengthen me,
And help me to live such a life so that someday – I will be with
You and her FOREVER!
AMEN

Who is She? – This Woman Called Mother
(Written as a Tribute to Mothers Everywhere)

Who is the woman we call mother? Well, we know that she has
certain supernatural powers:

- ➤ She can see through closed doors;
- ➤ She can hear your telephone conversation from the other side of the house;
- ➤ Many times, she knows what you are going to say before you say it;
- ➤ And what is even scarier, she knows what you are thinking.
- ➤ She knows when you are in pain and hurting – even if you are on the other side of the country. And, she is hurting, too.
- ➤ And it is true, Mothers do have eyes in the back of their heads – and they see everything you do.

But who is she?

- ➤ Abraham Lincoln, the 16th President of the U.S. said, "All that I am or hope to be, I owe to my mother."

➢ D.L. Moody, successful businessman turned American evangelist in the 19ᵗʰ century said, "All that I have ever accomplished in life, I owe to my mother."

➢ The inventor, Thomas Edison said, "My mother was the making of me."

➢ The industrialist and philanthropist, Andrew Carnegie said, "I am deeply touched by the remembrance of the one to whom I owe everything…"

But who is she?

➢ In Genesis 3:20, "And Adam called his wife's name Eve, because she was the mother of all living." KJV

➢ In Genesis 17:16, God told Abraham of his wife, Sarah, - "and she shall be a mother of nations; kings of people shall be of her." KJV

➢ Exodus 20:12 tells us, no – it **commands** us to honor her.

➢ In John 19:27, Jesus tells John to "Behold thy mother." KJV

➢ And to whom did God commit the care and early training of His only begotten Son? Did you ever think about that? God could have just put His Son on earth as a grown man. But he entrusted Him to this woman, who Jesus called **Mother.**

Well, let's see – who is she?

➢ One author writes, "more even than the father, the mother molds the life, character, and destiny of man. Every stage and phase of life is touched and influenced by her. Infancy, childhood, youth, adulthood, and old age alike look to her for inspiration: thus, she is both the morning and the evening star of life."

➢ Another writes, "It has been truly said that the home is the primeval school, the best, the most hallowed, and the most potential of all academies, and that mother is the first, the most influential, and therefore, the most important of all teachers."

➤ Mothers have an awesome responsibility, for as another writes, "No position in life is superior to that of the mother, no influence more potent for good or evil."

(All quotes taken from Bible Readings for the Home Circle, 1914 Edition)
So, who is she?

➤ She is the one who knows our heart, soul and mind and provides comfort in the time of need.
➤ She is the one to whom we owe everything – including life itself.
➤ She is the one who gave birth to nations; to kings; and to the Son of the maker of all and giver of all things.
➤ She is our teacher; our inspiration.
➤ She is Mother; There is no other…

It's Been So Long, But It Seems Just Like Yesterday
*(Written on the occasion of the twenty-fifth
anniversary of my mother's death…)*

*Always there with words of advice,
Always there, no matter the price.
Always giving and forgiving
It's as if she is still among the living.
Her face, her voice, her walk, her smile
It seems like yesterday, but it has been awhile.*

*We love you more than we did then
And each day we feel the love from Heaven you send
Thoughts of you are always on our mind*

As you continue to guide us, a sweet peace to find.
We pray that we will live our lives in such a way
That we will join You, Brother and Daddy someday

It's been so long, but it seems just like yesterday!

Essie M. Young
Wife, Mother, Educator, Church Worker

I am on the Battlefield
for My Lord

I am on the battlefield for my Lord,
I am on the battlefield for my Lord,
And I promised Him that I would serve Him till I die,
I am on the battlefield for my Lord.
(Written by Sylvana Bell & E.V. Banks;
Arranged by Thomas A. Dorsey)

In 1979, Daddy compiled and had published a collection of what he called – *Old Fashion Songs and Hymns as Sung by Black Folks.* The compilation contained the words to more than 130 songs; many familiar hymns of the church, such as *Just a Closer Walk with Thee; Can't Beat God's Giving; God Will Take Care of You; and He'll Understand and Say Well Done.* There were also songs I don't think you will find in any AME Hymn book or any other hymnal for that matter. Songs like: *Ninety-Nine and a Half* and *The Royal Telephone.* And, of course the booklet contained Daddy's favorite – *I am on the Battlefield for My Lord.* These were the songs sang at your grandmother or great-grandmother's church – that one room, wood frame structure that sat out in the middle of the woods. Songs that your ancestors sang from their souls with little or no instrumental accompaniment. Songs that lifted your spirits and caused you to want to just praise the Lord all day and night. Songs sung by Black Folks.

In Daddy's booklet as well as in the AME Hymnal there are only three verses and a chorus to *I am on the Battlefield*. But when Daddy sang this song, it could go on for days. I don't know if he just made the verses up as he went along, or if these were actually words to the song that he had learned as a child in his grandfather's church way out somewhere in the woods in Dermott, Arkansas. This hymn actually became Daddy's theme song. Even after he retired, on the first Sunday of each month – Communion Sunday – after communion and just before the benediction, the choir director would bring the microphone to Daddy who after retirement always sat on the first pew on the left-hand side of the church. The choir and congregation would begin singing the chorus to *I am on the Battlefield* and then Daddy would sing the verses. I think each time he sang at least six verses.

It was therefore fitting and appropriate that for the recessional for his Homegoing Service the choir and congregation sang *"I am on the Battlefield for My Lord."*

The last song in Daddy's booklet was one he wrote himself entitled, *"God's Going to Take Care of The Situation Afterwhile,"* and just like his version of *I am on the Battlefield,* and in true R.K. Young style, there are ten verses. He wrote this song to explain it all – in the same way that God took care of the situation for all of his people in the Bible, He will continue to take care of His people today.

"God's Going to Take Care of the Situation Afterwhile"
By Rufus King Young, Sr.

1. Moses standing at the Red Sea,
   The children all preparing to flee,
   Moses stood, lifted up his rod,
   With unshakable faith in God,
   For God's going to take care of the situation afterwhile.

   <u>CHORUS</u>
   God's going to take care of the situation afterwhile,
   God's going to take care of the situation afterwhile,
   It makes no difference how the way may be,
   For God's going to take care of the situation afterwhile.

2. Daniel thrown into the Lion's Den
   Being faithful unto the end.
   God came down, and locked the Lion's mouth
   While King Darius paced the floor of his house
   God's going to take care of the situation afterwhile.

3. Three Hebrew children in the fire
   On the fourth man they did rely
   Walking around Him they could sing
   Not a hair on them being singed
   God's going to take care of the situation afterwhile.

4. Jesus praying in Gethsemane
   Disciples giving no sympathy
   Angels came down and gave him strength
   To stand up in the judgment
   For God's going to take care of the situation afterwhile.

5. Jesus standing in Pilate's Court
   Pilot called on the people to vote,
   Jesus standing there held his peace
   "Crucify Him," rang without cease.
   God's going to take care of the situation afterwhile.

6. Plodding along toward Calvary,
   Simon helping Him bear the tree,
   A black man bore the cross that day
   And black men bear the cross today.
   But God's going to take care of the situation afterwhile.

7. Hanging there upon the cross
   Seemed like everything was loss
   Jesus Christ the Son of man
   Trusted everything in God's hand
   For God's going to take care of the situation afterwhile.

8. Friday and Saturday all was gloom
   Jesus Christ buried in the tomb
   Early Sunday angels came down
   The glory of heaven shone all around
   For God took care (care) of the situation on that day.

9. Paul and Silas were bound in jail,
   No word of cheer by friend or mail,
   Facing hell, they were unafraid,
   As the one to the other said…
   God's going to take care of the situation afterwhile.

10. Cheer up Christians, do not faint,
    At any picture Satan may paint,
    You may wade through seas of blood,
    But God's love will keep out the flood.
    For God's going to take care of the situation afterwhile.

CHORUS

God's going to take care of the situation afterwhile,
God's going to take care of the situation afterwhile,
It makes no difference how the way may be,
For God's going to take care of the situation afterwhile.

Daddy continued on the battlefield until the very end. Nothing could slow him down. In 1998 Daddy suffered a mild stroke, which required him to use a walker to get around. The first time I saw Daddy with his walker was when I finally realized that Daddy was getting old. Mommy had gone much too soon; she was only 62 years old at the time of her death. Mommy had been sick, suffering from diabetes, most of her adult life. Daddy always seemed to be the strong one, even though he too developed Type 2 diabetes. In my mind, Daddy was invincible. When it hit me that he too was just a man, it was like a child coming to the realization that there is no Santa Claus, Easter Bunny or Tooth Fairy. It was like a myth had just been dispelled.

Even though he had suffered a stroke and his mobility was limited, his memory remained intact and remarkable. He could still recall dates, places, people and events with ease. The stroke did not prevent him from participating in his favorite pastime – gardening. In retirement, he spent most of his time in his garden. With his walker and a folding chair, he continued to toil the soil and grow his favorite vegetables. We would often have to make him come into the house when it was getting dark. Did I say make him? – You couldn't **make** my father do anything he didn't want to do. He loved gardening. I truly believe that when he was toiling the land, he felt closer to God. He spent hours in his garden up until the very end.

Unfortunately, Dad did not live long enough to see the election of this nation's first Black President. However, I don't have to wonder what his reaction would have been. I know that he was in line with me when I cast my ballot. I also don't have to wonder how he would feel and what his reaction would be to the state of affairs in America today – the senseless killings of Blacks by the very people we pay to protect us; the separation of families seeking a better life for themselves; the devaluation of human life on so many levels. Yes, I know that R. K. Young would still be on the battlefield, and would still be on God's side.

James Robert recently said to me that with some preachers their style supersedes the substance of what they have to say. Well, Daddy certainly had style. His somewhat quiet demeanor; his easygoing charm; the resonance of his voice; and the slow and deliberate pace of his delivery was sure to catch your attention and make you pay attention. And of course, up until the very end, *he always had something to say.* And if you were wise, you would listen.

Pictures from Daddy's Ninetieth Birthday Party

Rev. Rufus King Young – Servant Leader, Builder

The Younguns (and Their Younguns) - Then and Now

--------------------------------∞--------------------------------

Essie Mae Laura Elizabeth attended Morris Brown College in Atlanta, GA (class of 1962). It was while she was there in school that she met and married Richard Norman. She married after her junior year in college and Mommy made Richard promise that she would complete her college education, which she did. Emley and Richard have one son, Richard, Jr. Richard, Jr. received his undergraduate degree from Clark Atlanta University. Emley worked for almost thirty-three years with the federal government in the Social Security Administration. Her husband died in 2009 and Emley and her son still live in Atlanta.

Rufus King, Jr. attended Wilberforce University in Wilberforce, Ohio. He graduated in 1964 with a degree in mathematics. He married his college sweetheart, Elouise Best and they have three children – Rufus King, III, Tia Yvette, and Terrance (Terry) Alexander. Rufus, Jr. spent a career working for Lockheed Aircraft. Rufus, Jr. died in 2002 after a brief illness. His oldest son Rufus, III (who we call Tookie) received an Associate's Degree from Clayton Junior College and completed his undergraduate work at Southern College of Technology. Tookie is married to the former Adrianne Lewis and they have twins, a boy and a girl – Jordan and Taylor, and live in Savannah, GA. Tia attended the University of Georgia in Athens, GA. She has one daughter, Zoe. Terry completed an Associate's degree from the Atlanta Arts Institute. Tia, Zoe, Terry and Rufus' widow, Elouise still live in Atlanta.

James Robert received his undergraduate degree from Texas Southern University (class of 1968); his Masters of Divinity from the Interdenominational Theological Seminary in Atlanta, GA; and his Doctorate Degree in Sociology of Religion from Boston University. While completing his doctoral studies he married Dorene Wells. James Robert retired in 2012 after a distinguishing teaching career at various colleges and universities in the New Hampshire/Massachusetts area including Middlesex Community College, Bentley University, University of Massachusetts Lowell, Rivier University and St. Anselm College. He also pastors the New Rye Union Congregational Church (known as the little white church on the hill). James Robert and Dorene have two children: Son - James, Jr (Jamey), who completed his undergraduate work at Dartmouth and has one Master's Degree from Harvard and another Master's Degree from Princeton. Their daughter, Alicia completed her undergraduate work at Brown University. Alicia is living and working in Boston. Jamey is married to Cara Berry and they have a daughter, Aurora. They live in Worcester, MA. James Robert lost his wife, Dorene in 2018. He still lives in Epsom, New Hampshire.

Ellen Arneatha Verdia graduated from Fisk University (class of 1970) and received a Master's Degree in Speech and Hearing Science from Vanderbilt University, both in Nashville, TN. After graduating from Fisk, Ellen married Tyrone Fizer, her college sweetheart. While living in Nashville, Ellen was on the faculty at Fisk University and worked for the State of Tennessee. Ellen and Tyrone have two daughters, Shelby and Selena. The family moved to the Washington, DC area in late 1979. Ellen worked for twenty-five years with the Department of Human Resources for Fairfax County Public Schools. Their oldest daughter, Shelby attended Hampton University and has a Master's Degree from University of Phoenix. Shelby has one son, Omavi, and they live in Baltimore, MD. Selena completed her undergraduate degree at Clark Atlanta University; her Master's Degree in Counseling from Howard University; and her Doctorate of Education from Bowie State University. Selena is married to Mark Muse and they have one son, Quincy; they live in Springdale, MD. Ellen and Tyrone live in Brandywine, MD about 20 miles outside Washington, DC.

Allena Anne also graduated from Fisk University (class of 1973) and later obtained a Master's Degree in Elementary Education from Oklahoma City University. In 1977 she married Rev. Leodis Strong and they have three children: Leodis Adam (whom we call Adam) is a graduate of the University of Central Oklahoma; Lela Eslanda (the proper name for Essie) received her undergraduate degree from Spelman College and Master's Degree from Georgia State University; and Bethany also received her undergraduate degree from Spelman College, a Doctorate of Medicine from Harvard University, and a Master's degree in Epidemiology from the University of Maryland. Bethany has become the family's first medical doctor. Allena spent a career as a public-school teacher in Nashville, North Carolina and Oklahoma. She lives in Oklahoma as does her son Adam. Lela is married to Adrian Holloway, M.D. They live in Baltimore, MD and have one daughter, Zuri; and Bethany completed her residency at Brigham-Women Hospital in Boston, MA, and has begun a fellowship at the University of Maryland Medical Center in Baltimore, MD.

Daddy and his two oldest Great-Grandchildren
Omavi and Zoe

The Man Who Had
Something to Say

Rufus King Young, Sr.
Born May 13, 1911 (Drew County, Arkansas); Died August 29, 2004 (North Little Rock, Arkansas)

Parents:
Robert and Laura Scott Young

Education:
Early education - Chicot County Training School, Dermott, AR; Associate of Arts Degree and Bachelor of Arts Degree – Shorter College, North Little Rock, AR; Bachelor of Divinity Degree – Payne Theological Seminary, Wilberforce University, Wilberforce, Ohio; Additional Studies at Chicago University

Reverend Young was licensed to preach by the African Methodist Episcopal Church in 1924 at the age of 12 and received his first pastoral appointment at the age of 18. He was ordained an Elder in 1934 and pastored churches in Arkansas, Mississippi, Alabama and Louisiana. During his tenure, he pastored Rosa Parks (St. Paul A.M.E. Church, Montgomery, AL - 1950-51) and Daisy Bates (*see The Long Shadow of Little Rock,* Daisy Bates, 1962). He played an active role in the March on Washington and the integration of Little Rock Central High School. Three of *the Little Rock Nine* were members of Bethel A.M. E. Church, where Dr. Young pastored for

33 years (1953-1986) – Ernest Green, Melba Pattillo and Gloria Ray. Dr. Young has been quoted as saying, "I saw my role as giving moral and spiritual undergirding to the civil rights movement and to those students who were under such severe pressure." And that he did. (See *Warriors Don't Cry,* Melba Pattillo Beals, 1994). Against the protest of some members, Rev. Young allowed the use of Bethel A.M.E. Church for some of the strategizing meetings.

Rev. Young was one of the few ministers who took a stand regarding the desegregation of the schools in Little Rock. In 1958, Rev. Young responded to a letter from Joshua Shepherd, Chair of the Committee for Arkansas Plan rejecting the committee's proposal that would require the Negroes to withdraw from Central High School. (University of Arkansas Libraries; Herbert Thomas Papers)

Pastorates:
- St. Peter AME Church, Lake Village, AR – 1929
- St. Peter AME Church, Gaines Landing and Parnell, AR – 1930-31
- St. Paul AME Church, Baxter, AR; and Soldier's Rest AME Church, Collins, AR – 1931-33
- St. Andrew AME Church, Little Rock, AR – 1933-37
- Hair's Tabernacle AME Church, Jackson, MS – 1940-44
- Bethel AME Church, Baton Rouge, LA – 1944-46
- Pearl Street AME Church, Jackson, MS – 1946-48
- St. Paul AME Church, Montgomery, AL – 1950-51
- Visitors Chapel AME Church, Hot Springs, AR – 1951-53
- Bethel AME Church, Little Rock, AR – 1953-86

Educational Services:
- Dean, Edward W. Lampton School of Religion, Campbell College, Jackson, MS – 1940-44
- President, Daniel Payne College, Birmingham, AL – 1948-50

- Dean, Jackson Theological Seminary, Shorter College, North Little Rock, AR., beginning in 1983
- Teaching Positions: Campbell College, Daniel Payne College, Shorter College and public-school teaching positions in Baton Rouge, LA, Prattville, AL, Little Rock, North Little Rock and Pulaski County School Districts

At the 84th Session of the Central Arkansas Annual Conference, Twelfth Episcopal District, African Methodist Episcopal Church (October 13-17, 2004) as part of the Conference Resolution, a former student, Presiding Elder Curley Roberts gave reflection of his days at Jackson Theological Seminary in which he took a class in Homiletics under the late Rev. Dr. Rufus K. Young. He recalled that Rev. Young would start his class on time at 6:00 p.m. and would talk the whole period (6:00 p.m. –8:00p.m.) and then ask for questions. Needless to say, the questions and answers went on for two hours or longer, and someone would look at the clock and say, "It's 10 o'clock!" Rev. Young would then say, "Let us pray and we will see you on Wednesday." (The AME Christian Recorder, the AME Church Official Newsletter, 11/20/2004 Edition, AME Publishing House, Nashville, TN)

Honors, Special Recognitions and Achievements:
- Honorary Doctor of Humane Letters Degree, Morris Brown College, Atlanta, GA
- Honorary Doctor of Divinity Degrees from Payne Theological Seminary, Wilberforce University, Wilberforce Ohio; and Shorter College, North Little Rock, AR
- 1977 became the first Black President of the Little Rock Christian Ministerial Alliance
- The Christian Ministerial Alliance established a Dr. Rufus K. Young Humanitarian Award
- 2002 – Connor Chapel AME Church was renamed the Rufus Young African Methodist Episcopal Church in his

honor (Now the Rufus Young Christian Center, 2100 Main Street, Little Rock, AR)

Family:

While pastoring at Hair Tabernacle in Jackson, MS, Dr. Young met and married Essie Mae Adams (daughter of James and Edna Adams). To this union were born five children: Essie Mae Laura Elizabeth, Rufus King, Jr., James Robert, Ellen Arneatha and Allena Anne.

Dr. Young had one sister, Bertha V. Young Lewis, and two brothers, both of whom pre-deceased him – Theodore Young and Clifton Young. Dr. Young was also preceded in death by his wife of almost forty-two years, Essie Mae in 1983 and his oldest son, Rufus, Jr. in 2002. After retiring from Bethel AME Church in 1986, he married Yvonne Brunner of Baton Rouge, LA., who also preceded him in death in 2003.

Affiliations:

- Alpha Phi Alpha Fraternity
- National Association for the Advancement of Colored People (NAACP)
- Interdenominational Ministerial Alliance
- A.M.E. Ministerial Alliance
- Arkansas Council of Churches
- President of the Retired Ministers Fellowship
- Masonic Order, 32nd Degree

In 1979, Dr. Young compiled a booklet of *Old Fashion Songs and Hymns – As Sung by Black Folk.* Included in the booklet is his all- time favorite – "On the Battlefield," for which he sang the verses solo every first Sunday at Bethel AME Church after his retirement, while serving as Pastor Emeritus there. His favorite song was also sung as the processional hymn at his funeral, also held at Bethel AME Church. His booklet of Songs and Hymns also contains one written by Dr. Young entitled "God's Going to Take Care of the Situation Afterwhile."

After almost 63 years in the ministry, Dr. Young retired from the pulpit at the age of 75 in 1986. Upon his retirement, the members of Bethel AME Church held a huge retirement celebration in his honor at the Robinson Auditorium (September 26, 1986). Of the numerous congratulatory letters and citations received was one from Bill Clinton, then Governor of Arkansas. The Arkansas Gazette also did a featured article on Dr. Young, which included an in-depth interview with him and highlighted his long and prolific career. *("Pastor for 33 years at Bethel AME will preach his final sermon Sunday"* – Arkansas Gazette, September, 1986)

In 1997, marking the 40th anniversary of the integration of Central High School, a citywide Reconciliation Service was held at St. Andrews Cathedral in Little Rock. Dr. Young was invited to provide the Homily for this service. In his book, *My Father Said Yes (2008),* Dunbar H. Ogden, son of the late Rev. Dunbar Ogden, Jr. who was the white Presbyterian Minister who led the Little Rock Nine up the steps of Central High School, recounts that memorable occasion and the words spoken by Dr. Young.

After Daisy Bates' death (November 4, 1999), a Memorial Service was held for her at the Robinson Auditorium in Little Rock (April 27, 2000). Dr. Young provided the opening remarks at this service and then President William Jefferson Clinton was the keynote speaker. He then delivered a message that set the tone for the day. *(His entire message is printed earlier in this book.)* In his speech, President Clinton commented "My old friend Reverend Young said about all that needs to be said." (Arkansas Democrat-Gazette, April 28 & 30, 2000)

In his later years, Dr. Young was much sought after for interviews and firsthand accounts of the civil rights movement in Arkansas. In the October 2002 edition of the Arkansas Tribune, in an article entitled, "Black Wisdom," Dr. Young told his story of the desegregation crisis at Central High School. Also, in 2002, Dr.

Young was featured in the documentary produced by the North American Mission Board of the Southern Baptist Convention entitled, *We Shall Not Be Moved*. The film was narrated by Ossie Davis and documented the role of the African American church in the civil rights movement.

Dr. Young died peacefully on August 29, 2004 in his home in North Little Rock, AR. His wake was held at the Rufus Young AME Church and the funeral service was held at Bethel AME Church on September 4, 2004. He was eulogized by his second son, the Rev. Dr. James Robert Young, Sr. Dr. Rufus King Young, Sr. was laid to rest next to his beloved wife and mother of his children, Essie Mae Adams Young at the Haven of Rest Cemetery in Little Rock, which is also the resting place for Daisy Bates, and other notable Black Arkansans such as Scipio A. Jones and Joseph Booker.

Many of Rev. Young's papers were donated to the Butler Center so that they could be preserved. On Friday, February 17, 2012, The Butler Center for Arkansas Studies held a reception to dedicate this collection of works. The collection includes family documents, correspondence, photographs, school and church related materials including sermons, programs, and ministerial association minutes. The Butler Center for Arkansas Studies is a department of the Central Arkansas Library System (CALS), and was created in 1997 through an endowment by the late Richard C. Butler Sr. for the purpose of promoting a greater understanding and appreciation of Arkansas history, literature, art, and culture. The collection is open to the public and information can be found at the following website: http://arstudies.contentdm.oclc.org/cdm/singleitem/collection/findingaids/id/1124/rec/2

A biography of Rev. Young can also be found in the *Encyclopedia of Arkansas History and Culture* - located at: http://www.encyclopediaofarkansas.net/encyclopedia/entry-detail.aspx?entryID=8264

Rev. R. K. Young's biography is also included in The *Encyclopedia*

<u>of African Methodism – Bicentennial Edition 1816-2016,</u> published in 2019

All photos are from the Young family photo collection. Some may have been taken by the late Ralph Armstrong.

From the R.K. Young Family Archives are the following:
- Family Tree of the Young and Adams Families – researched and prepared by R. K. Young
- Letter written by R.K. Young regarding the integration of Central High School
- Christmas Letter sent by R.K. Young the first Christmas after his wife's death

Rev. Rufus King Young, Sr.
Pastor, Preacher, Educator, Civil Rights Activist,
Religious and Community Leader

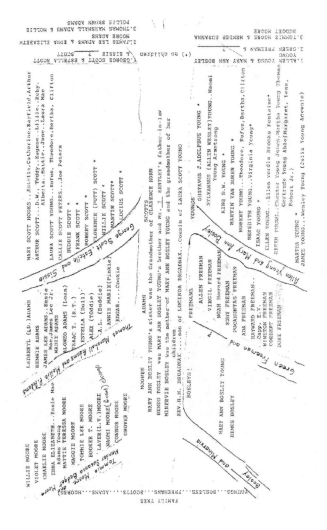

April 23, 1958

Committee For Arkansas Plan
Mr. Joshua K. Shepherd, Chairman
P. O. Box 1837
Little Rock, Arkansas

Dear Mr. Shepherd:

    This comes to acknowledge receipt of your letter as of April 7, 1958 containing a copy of the proposal which Mr. Herbert L. Thomas, Sr. presented to the State Board of Education for consideration as a means of working toward a solution of our perplex school problem in the area of segregation or integration. As suggested in your letter, I shared the proposal with the leaders in our church and got their reactions. Our Trustee Board at its regular monthly meeting took the plan under consideration. They were impressed with the sincerity and conscienceness on the part of Mr. Thomas in his effort to find a solution to the problem, and we wish to commend him for his noble undertaking for we feel that such efforts to re-establish the lines of communication between the races should never be relinquished. However, the Board voted unanimously to oppose any plan that would have the Negroes withdrawn from Central High School.

    We truly hope that you will be able to understand our position in this particular instant and we will remain opened to further discussions or suggestions in this matter.

Sincerely and Prayerfully yours,

Rufus K. Young, Pastor

The Word became flesh and lived for a while among
John 1:14

1963   1983

120TH ANNIVERSARY
of
BETHEL A. M. E. CHURCH
CHRISTMAS GREETINGS

To The Beloved Members of The Bethel Family and Friends:

This is the first time in forty-two years that I have been without the
companionship of my beloved wife at this season of the year. She left
me and the other Youngers last February 26th to live forever with the
eternal Prince of Peace. It was she who coined the phrase "The R. K.
Youngs and their Youngums." The last Younger to arrive was James Robert
Young, Jr., who arrived March first of this year, three days after my
wife's passing, just in time for a picture of him to be buried with her.

So, "Through It all" which was one of my wife's favorite songs, and
with grateful thanks to you for all that you have done and are doing
to help share our loss and sorrow, I extend to you my warmest wishes
for a very Merry Christmas and a most happy, and Prosperous New Year!
May God ever bless you and cause his face to shine upon you and give
you Peace! Amen.

Your Chief Servant,

R. K. Young
Pastor Young

__Upon his retirement__ – "I have fought the good fight, I have finished the race, I have kept the faith, here at Bethel A.M.E. Church Little Rock for 33 years, 3 months and 3 weeks and now I am retiring." RKY, Sr.

I've Gone Home

It's been a long journey,
It's been a tough climb,
There've been lots of pain,
But I thank God for all the good time.

I've seen my share of sorrows,
Agony and woe.
But in the end
I thank God for every friend, and yes, even every foe.

For there was a lesson learned
In every traveled road.
It made me stronger, wiser...
A new blessing with every seed sowed.

So, I thank God
For each day I spent
Growing, giving, loving...
Sometimes not knowing why I was sent.

But the journey's over
And now I know.
It was all worth the struggle
As Home I go.

So, cry if you must
But let them be tears of joy and glee
I lived a good life
And now my Father has called for me.

Once you begin to reflect
In solitude, so your mind won't roam
Know that I am at peace
Because - I've gone Home.
eavyf

Printed in the United States
By Bookmasters